WOODLANDER

A GUIDE TO SUSTAINABLE
WOODLAND MANAGEMENT

WOODLANDER

A GUIDE TO SUSTAINABLE WOODLAND MANAGEMENT

BEN LAW

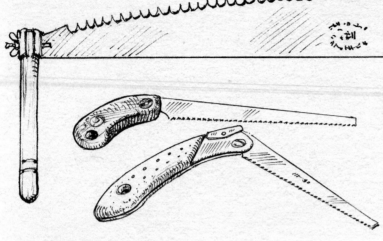

CONTENTS

'*The hazel tree did not belie its name today. The whole of the copse-wood
where the mist had cleared returned purest tints of that hue, amid which
Winterborne himself was in the act of making a hurdle, the stakes being
driven firmly into the ground in a row, over which he bent and wove the
twigs. Beside him was a square, compact pile like the alter of Cain, formed
of hurdles already finished, which bristled on all sides with the sharp
points of their stakes. Rows of brushwood lay on the ground as it had
fallen under the axe; and a shelter had been constructed near at hand,
in front of which burnt the fire...*'

From *The Woodlanders* by Thomas Hardy

'As Woodlanders, we have a responsibility to enhance the biodiversity of our forests, to ensure species as well as ourselves can survive and thrive.'

Introduction

At a crucial time in our understanding as a species on this planet, and with climate change now the biggest threat we face looking into the future, our relationship with trees and woodlands and their growth and survival is tied symbiotically with our own. By reading this book, I hope you will discover a new relationship with trees and woodlands, whether as an owner, or through a more recreational connection.

In this book, we go on a journey to gain an understanding of the woodland landscape and the biodiversity of its habitat. This will help us make good long-term decisions on woodland management, with a balanced view of species conservation, timber production and the importance of woodlands to our well-being. I have focused on small woodlands, as there are many of these that need caring for and there is a growing number of people who are becoming small woodland owners.

How we can help

For many of us, climate change can feel overwhelming when we consider the vast industrial wastelands we have created and that we now need to change to clean-energy producing environments. It is easy to feel disempowered as individuals,

but tree planting and creating new woodlands is something we can all become involved in – in turn, we can feel part of a movement towards positive change. Diversity, species choice for planting new woodlands and how to turn that monocultural arable field into a thriving biodiverse woodland for future generations is all within our reach.

As woodlanders, we have a responsibility to enhance the biodiversity of our forests, to ensure species as well as ourselves can survive and thrive. With good observation, surveying and thoughtful planning, we can create and look after multifunctional woodlands where biodiversity increases, timber for construction and craftwork can be harvested and we can enjoy the clean air for a range of diverse educational and recreational activities.

TYPES OF WOODLAND

In this chapter, I categorize woodlands into different types. This is a starting point for gaining an understanding of your woodland. The age of it and how it has been managed often form the guidelines in terms of woodland type.

Ancient woodland

The woodlands of Great Britain are part of what we refer to as deciduous temperate forest, which stretches across Europe into Asia and runs north to south, from the southern edges of Scandinavia to the Mediterranean. The exception is the Caledonian Forest in the Highlands of Scotland, which forms part of the boreal coniferous forest stretching across Scandinavia into Russia.

The term ancient woodland is used to describe a woodland known to have been in existence continuously for 400 years or more (since 1600 in England and Wales) and 250 years or more (since 1750) in Scotland. Planting trees was uncommon 400 years ago, so it can be presumed that most of these woodlands developed naturally, containing soils undisturbed for hundreds of years.

Ancient woodland establishment

What is referred to as the UK's native tree species only colonized Great Britain after the Ice Age, forming as the ice retreated and the climate warmed. The process of woodland establishment at this time seems to follow the process of natural regeneration we see today. This process begins with the pioneer species such as birch and alder, which establish and grow quickly and then are succeeded by the slower-growing, longer-living species such as oak, beech and yew.

These slower-growing species form the canopy. We refer to these as the climax species because other species do not succeed them. They will die or blow over in a storm and then, with light reaching the forest floor, the process of regeneration begins again. Over time, the process of succession ensures the climax species form the canopy again.

Spring highlights the diverse ground flora in ancient woodland.

Bluebells, an ancient woodland indicator plant, brighten the transition into spring.

SMALL WOODLANDS

When referring to small woodlands, these are areas of 61.5 acres (25ha) or less. Small woodlands make up 25 per cent of woodland cover in the UK, or 1,042,785 acres (422,000ha). Small woodlands are not a type of woodland in their own right but are of interest due to their size, their often non-commercial nature and their diversity of ownership and management. Small woods may be ancient woodland, coppice or a plantation, or a mixture of any of the woodland types.

A thriving ecology

The build-up of decaying wood in ancient woodlands creates a unique habitat for fungi and invertebrates. The plant species that can be found in these woodlands are often unique to woodland environments and cannot survive in more exposed conditions.

Ancient woodlands are a treasured seed bank and ecological resource. They are a place of learning, containing and maintaining the biological and cultural history of the past 400 years or more.

A visit to an ancient woodland is food for the soul. I recommend taking the time to research and find them near to where you live. Every woodland is unique and has its own balance of biodiversity and cultural history, and can give you an insight into species that have thrived on your local soils and an opportunity to take time to stop and observe.

The colourful fly agaric Amanita muscaria appears in the autumn. Note: this species is defined as poisonous.

A VISIT TO KINGLEY VALE

A visit to an ancient woodland is for me both a journey of wonder and an education in the evolution of our landscape. I have visited Kingley Vale National Nature Reserve near Chichester in West Sussex, UK, on a number of occasions and it never fails to inspire me. The ancient yew trees that have colonized the lower levels are true examples of the wonder and complexity of how old trees grow and survive. Kingley Vale offers so much more than being the largest yew forest in Europe, with its Bronze Age burial mounds, butterfly-filled chalk grasslands and stunning views across Bosham Harbour and out to the Isle of Wight.

But admire as I do the stunning views and the flitting of the chalkhill blue butterflies, they are to me just a sideshow for the ancient yews that stretch out in the lower reaches of the coombe. These trees, often hidden among the woodland and scrub, are prolific in number and, walking down a tiny pathway, one emerges in a cathedralesque clearing with the spreading limbs of an ancient yew stretching many yards across the forest. The lack of vegetation and other plant life around the yews adds to their majestic appearance.

I always feel it a privilege to spend time in the company of ancient trees: it is humbling to be in the presence of an individual tree that may have been growing on the same spot for over 1,000 years. It brings our own short life span into perspective. A visit to an ancient woodland should be educational and a time for reflection. It is an opportunity to pause and appreciate a landscape that has survived through all that human evolution has thrown at it and which has, to some degree, helped shape it. It is a reminder that, as we plant new woodlands and help create the landscapes of the future, we must also think long-term and plan way beyond our own lifetime.

Looking down on part of the yew forest at Kingley Vale.

One of the many ancient yew trees at Kingley Vale.

Wood pasture

Wood pasture describes a landscape of widely spaced trees that are undergrazed by large herbivores such as sheep or cows. In fact, it can be seen as the influence for a number of agroforestry systems that involve trees and other crops or trees and livestock integrated into one system. For example, a silvopastoral system could involve sheep and geese grazing under standard walnut trees.

The decline of wood pastures

A lot of the UK's 'commons' – land that wasn't closed off for private use – were once wood pastures where commoners had rights to graze livestock and collect firewood. Many of these commoners' rights were lost during Enclosure, when landholdings were turned into larger farms and restricted from use as common land, from about the thirteenth century onwards. This has affected the social balance of land, ownership and shared usage of land with the once-shared commons now mainly in the sole ownership of large estates and individual landowners.

Pollarding

Pollarding is an important silvicultural practice for wood pastures as the regrowth after cutting is at a height beyond the reach of grazing animals. Pollarding trees and allowing the timber to lie on the ground allows grazing livestock to gain minerals from the bark before the trees are collected for firewood. This, in turn, creates a unique forest habitat that allows trees and grazing animals to thrive symbiotically.

Pollarding cycle

FAR LEFT: Pollarded willows that are undergrazed with sheep.

REWILDING

The work of the Dutch ecologist Frans Vera has challenged the presumptions of how forests have evolved since the last Ice Age. His vision is based on wider-spaced trees with larger mammals grazing in a landscape of grassland and trees. The lack of predator species for the large mammals means that humans need to cull a percentage of the larger mammals to keep numbers in balance.

Rewilding, in its purest form, encourages humans to step back and allow nature to rebalance. They become a small part, rather than a dominant force, in the landscape. Provided large enough areas can become rewilding zones, this is an exciting change and should have a positive impact.

Knepp Wildland is an experimental rewilding project in Sussex, UK, based on the work of Frans Vera. This 3,500-acre (1,416-ha) estate has five species of megafauna and still has a 'farming' element to the project with sales of organic meat. Early biodiversity results are very encouraging, with nightingales and purple emperor butterflies utilizing the site. I have visited Knepp a few times and I have no doubts about its value as a future wildlife and biodiversitry site, although

I observe with interest the balance needed to allow natural regeneration of trees within the system. Experimental projects such as Knepp may well guide some of our future forest-management systems.

Old English longhorn cattle at Knepp play an important role in ground disturbance and seed transportation.

Coppice woodland

Coppicing is a traditional form of woodland management that has been practised for at least 1,000 years. Coppicing involves the successional cutting of broadleaf woodland during the dormant winter period. In spring, when the sap rises, the stump (referred to as the stool) sends out shoots of new growth. These shoots are encouraged to grow on until they reach an appropriate size and diameter for using the timber. They are cut again during the dormant winter period and the process repeats itself.

The wood cut during coppicing is used for craft produce, fencing, building products and wood fuel. Coppicing prior to the 1950s supported a large rural workforce, but with the arrival of plastics and the need to rebuild large parts of the country after the Second World War, the industry declined. It is currently seeing some revival as the desire for craft and sustainable products is on the increase. This will help reverse the loss of many habitats that the decline in coppicing affected.

The coppicing cycle

Cutting coppice on a regular cycle creates a patchwork of areas in a woodland, each at a different stage of regrowth. These areas create different habitats for different species, which move with the coppice worker from area to area. The freshly cut areas of coppice produce a flush of wildflowers – these plants have adapted to the cyclical pattern of shade and light provided by the regular and repeated cutting patterns of the coppice worker. Many of these plants are important food plants for butterflies

and the decline in particular woodland butterfly species can be correlated with the decline of regular coppicing.

Coppicing is one of the rare patterns in nature where humans are an important part of the ecosystem. By cutting the coppice, humans are creating the patchwork of habitat so vital to so many species, and in return they are gaining materials to build and make craft produce. Take the human element out and the coppice becomes overstood, the plants are shaded out and biodiversity decreases.

ABOVE LEFT: Coppiced woodland at Prickly Nut Wood showing sweet chestnut coppice with three years of regrowth in the foreground and 27 years beyond.

TOP RIGHT: The multiple stems arising from one stool of coppiced sweet chestnut.

ABOVE: Dog violet and wood anemone spring into life after this hazel coppice has been cut.

A good-quality oak standard, formed through the management of the surrounding coppice.

Coppice with standards

Many coppice woodlands also have larger standard trees growing amongst the coppice. These trees add another layer to the woodland, creating habitat for many species of invertebrates, butterflies and birds. Standards are often different species to the main area of coppice.

Oak standards over hazel coppice is a traditional system. Typically, the oak standards were managed by the coppice worker for creating curves and braces used in ship- and house building. Managing the growing pattern of the coppice to help create the shape of a curve would often take over one hundred years, so it could be the grandchild of the original coppice worker who felled the standard tree. The main stem of the standard, well shaded by the coppice for most of its life, would often produce a good-quality, knot-free piece of timber for sawing into planks.

Maintaining standards

Standards need to be well managed, otherwise the coppice below will receive restricted light. This means the coppice regrowth, searching for light, grows in an irregular pattern and does not produce the straight poles that the craftsperson needs for their work. The ideal canopy cover of standards over coppice is about 10–15 per cent.

Many coppices become neglected (or overstood) due to the standards getting too large and the quality of the coppice below deteriorating. Coppice workers are often only trained to fell small-diameter trees or do not have the equipment needed to deal with standards. Standards with large spreading crowns should be removed and, over many coppice cycles, it should be possible to encourage a mixture of ages in standards, from maturing established trees through to young standards at the start of their lives. A well-managed coppice-with-standards woodland offers more biodiversity than a pure coppice one.

ABOVE: Oak standard over hazel coppice.

Woodlander's story: the nightjar

Each year towards the end of May, as the first warm evenings are upon us, I anticipate the return of the nightjar. This migratory bird makes its journey each year from sub-Saharan Africa to Prickly Nut Wood. Coppiced woodlands are not the first choice of habitat for the nightjar; they prefer open heathland. However, with the lack of suitable sites, the nightjar has adapted to the coppice, provided there is an open and freshly cut area. I leave standing deadwood as calling posts around and among the coppice and, for the past 28 summers, the nightjar has returned.

As the light begins to vanish, the quiet of the evening is broken with the vibrating 'churring' call of the nightjar. It is the male who arrives first, often a week to ten days before the female. It is a haunting and unique sound and to me heralds the transition from spring to summer.

The nightjar descends from his perch, swooping across the freshly cut coppice. The wings slap together above its body, making a clapping sound followed by the familiar 'co-ic' call. The 'churring' continues at dawn and dusk, increasing in intensity after the females have arrived.

The two eggs are laid on the ground, a few scratches on the soil the only markers of the nest site – the nightjar relies on camouflage for its protection. If it is a very warm summer, it might consider a second brood. By the end of August all is quiet and the nightjar returns to Africa.

Short-rotation coppice

There are a number of species that are grown on a short rotation for a particular end use. With traditional crafts, where small-diameter stems are needed, coppice is cut on a short cycle of between one to four years to provide the raw material for the craft worker to weave or work into the finished product.

Species grown on short rotation

The osier willow (*Salix viminalis*), almond willow (*Salix triandra*) and the purple willow (*Salix purpurea*) are all cut on an annual cycle for basketry. Basket making is globally one of the most ancient of crafts and the need for wetlands to successfully grow osier beds has seen much of the industry in England being based around the Somerset Levels. Some willow growers in the Levels have more than 50 different varieties of willow, adding a variety of colour and form for the basket maker to work with. Varieties of these three species are cultivated and sold by the weighed bundle. Modern hybrid varieties of willow and poplar are grown on a short rotation of one to four years for biomass production.

They are harvested, chipped and fed into biomass woodchip boilers. These hybrid varieties have very high growth rates, often reaching more than 15ft (4.5m) in a year – they are also referred to as 'biomass forestry'.

Sweet chestnut has its heartland in the south-east, with the majority of the UK's coppiced sweet chestnut being found in Sussex, Surrey and Kent. Although mainly cut on longer cycles, some areas are cut on a three-year short rotation coppice cycle for walking sticks. These are steam bent and have for many years been supplied to the NHS.

Osier beds, short-rotation willow coppice.

TREES THAT COPPICE OR SUCKER

When you cut a broadleaf tree in winter, most trees will coppice and send out new growth from the stem just below where you have cut it, but some trees will sucker. Trees that sucker send out their new growth from the roots of the existing tree and therefore can be a few yards away from the original cut stem. Most coniferous trees die when they are felled but there are a few exceptions.

TREES THAT COPPICE

Ash	*Fraxinus excelsior*
Field maple	*Acer campestre*
Hazel	*Corylus avellana*
Sweet chestnut	*Castanea sativa*
Alder	*Alnus glutinosa*
Hornbeam	*Carpinus betulus*
Silver birch	*Betula pendula*
Downy birch	*Betula pubescens*
Small-leaved lime	*Tilia cordata*
Goat willow	*Salix caprea*
English oak	*Quercus robur*
Holly	*Ilex aquifolium*
Yew	*Taxus baccata*
Beech	*Fagus sylvatica*
Coast redwood	*Sequoia sempervirens*

TREES THAT SUCKER

Aspen	*Populus tremula*
Wild service	*Sorbus torminalis*
Wild cherry	*Prunus avium*
Black locust	*Robinia pseudoacacia*
Blackthorn	*Prunus spinosa*
Bird cherry	*Prunus padus*

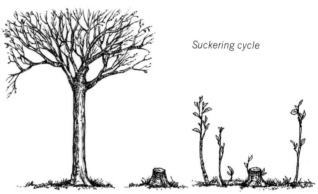

Suckering cycle

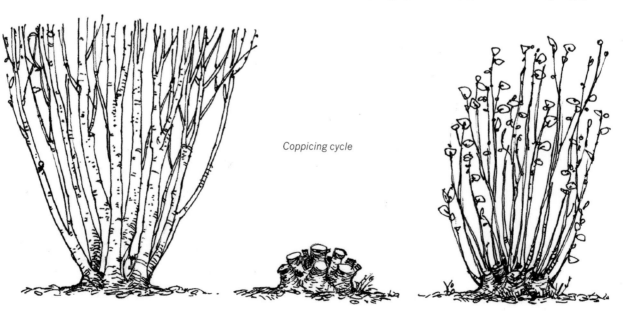

Coppicing cycle

Plantations

After the First World War, the Forestry Commission was set up to produce a new timber resource for the country after so many woodlands had been depleted for the war effort. To that goal, they succeeded and the industrial forestry model was born. Plantations can be coniferous, broadleaf or mixed and nowadays make up the majority of woodlands managed for timber production in Great Britain.

Although successful in producing timber, plantation forestry has often come at a cost to the environment. Large monocultural plantings have reduced the diverse habitats that a more traditional mixed high forest provided.

The silvicultural (the branch of forestry concerned with the cultivation of trees) practice of management ending with a large clearfell operation has caused much loss of valuable woodland soils on hillsides, with the soil eroding away to block up streams and rivers below. On flatter landscapes, soils have been affected from rising water levels following clearfell operations.

Plantations on an ancient woodland site (PAWS)

Many ancient woodlands were felled and replanted as plantations after the Second World War and over the following decades. The thinking behind this change was that ancient woodlands had no commercial value and by planting a fast-growing, usually coniferous, species the woodland would give a financial return to the landowner during their lifetime. This was at a time when words like biodiversity were not a forestry consideration and the decisions on land use were dominated by short-term economic gain.

Grants were available for planting the woodlands, mostly with heavy shading coniferous species – and this meant that the unique ground flora and associated

ABOVE: Clearfelling plantations on hillsides, like this in North Wales, risks soil erosion.

TOP RIGHT: Continuous cover forestry encourages diversity in species and age.

RIGHT: A plantation on an ancient woodland site.

fauna of the ancient woodland struggled to survive. Move forward to the current situation and grants are now available to remove the coniferous plantations from ancient woodland sites. The value of ancient woodlands is now being recognized and many have shown signs of recovery with dormant flora seed regenerating after the conifers have been removed.

Continuous cover forestry (CCF)

This type of forestry has been practised in Europe for many years but is in its infancy in Great Britain. CCF is a management practice ensuring a canopy is maintained across the woodland at multiple levels without the need for a clearfell. This involves an irregular forest structure, with particular trees or groups of trees being harvested once they have reached a commercial size for felling, and the encouragement of natural regeneration, with more diversity of tree species and age structure.

CCF can be a silvicultural practice in coniferous, broadleaf or mixed woodland. The move towards CCF and away from the clearfell practices of the past 100 years is a positive step in commercial forestry. What I find most encouraging is that young foresters will be learning about CCF at college and when their generation become the decision-makers on managing woodlands, the clearfell model will hopefully disappear.

Orchards

Traditional orchards with large trees grown above pasture are an important landscape feature and social resource. Orchards provide food, spring blossom, a habitat for insects and a valuable pollen source for bees. They are also an important landscape feature and a place to work and to gather socially, for picking and celebrating the harvest.

Mixed use with orchards

These traditional orchards not only produce fruit but can be undergrazed with poultry. Undergrazing with chickens and geese produces an extra food crop in the orchard and the poultry help with pest control, manuring and eating surplus windfalls. Such systems are based on trees grafted onto large rootstocks (such as M25 for apple trees – see table, right, for rootstocks). The rootstock will determine the eventual size of the fruit tree, how long it lives and how soon it produces fruit.

Although usually planted as a separate area from woodlands, it is possible to incorporate fruit trees into a woodland system. Crab apple (*Malus sylvestris*) and wild pear (*Pyrus communis*) can sometimes be found in ancient woodlands.

TYPES OF ROOTSTOCKS FOR ORCHARDS

The M before the number comes from the East Malling research station where these rootstocks originated. The rootstock affects the size, how soon the tree will fruit and its age. An M27 rootstock is weak and the tree will be short lived, whereas an M25 can form a large orchard tree that can be expected to still be producing 80 years after planting. The variety of tree, such as an 'Egremont Russet' or a 'Laxtons superb', is then grafted onto the rootstock to produce your chosen apple.

ROOTSTOCK	EFFECT ON TREE	STARTS FRUITING	HEIGHT
M27	Extremely dwarfing	2 years	4–6ft (1.2–1.8m)
M9	Dwarfing	2–3 years	6–8ft (1.8–2.4m)
M26	Dwarfing	2–3 years	8–10ft (2.4–3m)
MM106	Semi dwarfing	3–4 years	10–13ft (3–4m)
MM111	Vigorous	4–5 years	13–15ft (4–4.5m)
M25	Very vigorous	5–6 years	15ft plus (4.5m plus)

Woodlander's story: fruit in a forest

At Prickly Nut Wood, I have ancient crab apples growing on a traditional earthbank boundary between woodland compartments. In my book *The Woodland Way* I wrote about 'coppice fruit avenues' where I incorporated fruit trees (mainly apples) between cants of coppice. As the coppice is cut, more light reaches the fruit trees and in turn they produce a good crop of fruit.

After twenty years, I think a better description would be 'coppice fruit clusters' as small clusters of six to ten trees have done better than linear avenues. These apples are grown on large rootstocks and left unpruned after early formative work. I have a mixture of eaters, cookers and cider varieties grown this way. Closer to my house and workshop I have apple trees grafted onto medium rootstocks (MM106 and M11 – see table above), with very small M26 rootstocks used around the vegetable garden.

Traditional orchard on M25 rootstock in flower.

UNDERSTANDING YOUR WOODLAND

I spend a lot of my life in woodlands, not just living and working in my own but visiting other people's and advising on management strategies. The more time you spend in them, the more you will observe and understand, and the better your decision-making will become. In simple terms, you are learning to read the landscape. The assessment of your woodland is critical to making good management decisions for the future and helping you to understand its history and evolution. This process should not be rushed. Woodlands have often evolved over many hundreds of years and doing no practical management for a year – using that time to assess a woodland – is the minimum you should allocate.

Background research

Finding out any history you can about your woodland will complement the practical surveying work that goes on within the woodland itself. This can be done using a variety of maps. The first Ordnance Survey map was of the county of Kent, in 1801, primarily for military use with concerns of a French invasion, but most of Great Britain was mapped between 1840 and 1880. By checking the position of your woodland on these early maps, it will be possible to identify whether the land was woodland or agricultural land 150 years ago.

It is possible to view many of the old Ordnance Survey maps online – alternatively, county reference libraries or the county records office will usually have copies, but you may need to make an appointment as these items are not usually on display. Maps of artefacts (commonly referred to as bank and ditch maps) can also be found at the county records office and these can be useful for identifying old boundaries and archaeological features such as earthbanks and other artificially made earthworks. When considering maps, a visit to the interactive 'MAGIC' mapping website (see page 48) will give a variety of overlaying maps for the woodland that can help identify soil and geology, legal status, administrative boundaries and much more.

If possible before visiting a woodland, take a copy of an Ordnance Survey map of the area with you. This will help get a feel for how your woodland area sits within the landscape. It will tell you what type of landscape surrounds the woodland, if it is more woodland or arable land, and if there are buildings or water features. The area surrounding the woodland will have a direct impact on the woodland itself and the management decisions you will make after your year of observation. The map will also show you the current access routes to the woodland and any roadside access points.

Check your rights
Deeds of a woodland can also be useful for clarifying access tracks and any permitted access across land for extracting timber. It is not uncommon for a small woodland to have been sold off from a farm but with a condition in the deeds added to allow access at a particular time of year for the extraction of timber. If you are purchasing a woodland, check if you are also purchasing the sporting rights and mineral rights. If these are kept by the original owner, they will have rights to access your woodland for shooting or possibly to quarry beneath the woodland.

Ask local officers and residents
It is sensible to contact your local Forestry Commission officer as they may have information or a previous management plan of the woodland, which could be helpful in understanding the past patterns of management.

A large amount of useful information can be gained by talking to local people who have lived and worked in the area of the woodland. They will often remember new plantings, areas that were felled and approximately when and if areas of the woodland became flooded or very wet in winter. All of this can be gleaned by taking time to speak to a passing dog walker or over a pint in the local pub.

Look at the bigger picture
Small woodlands may have been created by splitting a large woodland into smaller segments. In this situation it is possible the woodland may be a small part of a larger plantation. Look at the surrounding woodland to get an understanding of whether the woodland was once part of a larger wood.

THIS PAGE: This extraction ride and diverse ground flora indicates recent use and ancient woodland origin.
OPPOSITE: Areas of multiple-stemmed trees shows evidence of previous coppicing.

The topography of the woodland becomes much clearer after an area is coppiced.

Observation

Assessing a woodland is a very different experience to assessing arable land. A 12.35-acre (5ha) arable field will have no visual constraints to the area except perhaps slope in the landscape. You will be able to view the area, make out the boundaries and get a feel for the topography in a short visit. The same size of woodland may be impenetrable in places, and standing at your chosen entry point may give you no view across the woodland. Finding the boundaries of the woodland could take an entire day. The woodland's topography will most likely be hidden from view by the varying height of trees and shrubs. You are about to enter a landscape often disguised from the outside.

Observation is your starting point for assessing a woodland. Each visit will build layer upon layer of the fabric and feel of the place and you will begin to build your understanding of the landscape. The more often you visit it, the clearer your knowledge and understanding of it will become.

Woodlands change dramatically throughout the seasons. Plants appear in spring that show no sign of life in the winter. Snow allows for clear tracking of animals and their chosen pathways. Migratory species may arrive in the summer and leave before autumn – all of these are part of the habitat of your woodland and, as a steward of your woodland, you need to know the species that live there or visit there so that your management decisions enhance rather than deplete its biodiversity.

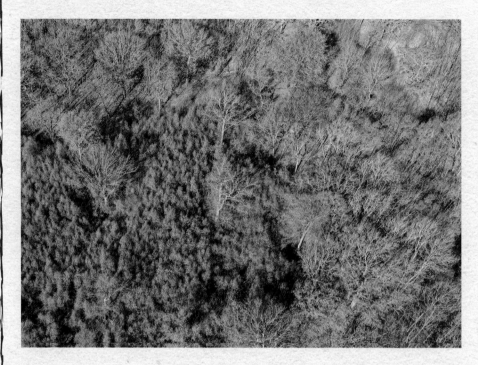

DRONES

The use of drones should be considered in assessing woodlands. A small drone with a good camera can give us a totally different perspective. The ability to look down from just above the canopy layer can be a useful tool in assessing the health of the woodland or particular trees. The drone can take still photographs or a video of the woodland, and give the owner extra information from which to make management decisions.

The green area of woodland shows hazel coppice just come into leaf. The photograph enables an accurate assessment of the canopy cover of the standards growing amongst it.

Woodlander's story: night-time observation

Night-time visits are important as well. Woodlands come alive at night. Sitting quietly beneath a tree in the middle of the woods will make you aware of the activity going on around you. I recommend a few camping weekends to observe evening, night-time and dawn activity. At Prickly Nut Wood in the summer, I can observe bats feeding over the pond at dusk and the sound of nightjars 'churring' and wing clapping in the areas of freshly cut coppice. A stroll down the main access track where it joins the field will often be lit by the bioluminescent beetles we refer to as glow-worms. Further into the night the sound of nightingales can be heard in the young coppice and the hooting of owls can reach a crescendo on a moonlit night, where a rare glimpse of a dormouse climbing through the hazel may be witnessed. All of these woodland inhabitants would be missed with only daytime observation.

Tawny owl.

First observational visit

Allow yourself the whole day so that you are not rushing to get back for a particular time. Without time constraints you will be able to absorb yourself in the woodland, get a feeling for the environment and become more in tune with the pace of the woods.

As you enter the woodland for the first time, there may be existing access tracks and these will allow you to enter with ease. Try and work your way around the boundaries, noting down flora and fauna that you recognize. Look out for earthbanks, ditches and any water features.

You might see flat, levelled-out areas where charcoal burning may have taken place, hollows where iron ore may have been extracted or a more rectangular hollow that may have been an old sawpit site. Old sawpits are usually sited near the edge of a ride.

Archaeology and history is under your feet. Be aware of the topography – is the land fairly flat? Or is it clearly sloping? Stop when you find a suitable spot, sit down and pour yourself a cup of tea and observe.

Allow the woodland to appear to you – don't force yourself upon it. Particular trees will stand out because they are old or unusual looking, perhaps thick with ivy or have a large broken branch. These trees will become your reference points. They will be the signposts you use when you return for your next visit. Slowly, visit by visit, the woodland will become more familiar. The signpost trees that helped you navigate on your early visits

will be more in the background and you will begin to notice the different layers in the woodland, the smaller trees and the ground flora.

Visit by visit, layer upon layer, your observation will help form your understanding of the woodland. The information you gather will allow you to make good decisions when preparing a management plan.

ABOVE LEFT: Charcoal burning.

ABOVE RIGHT: Site of an ancient sawpit – the name of this coppiced area is 'old sawpit piece'.

BELOW: A furnace pond forming part of the remains of a charcoal blast furnace from the Wealden iron industry.

FIRST VISIT: WHAT TO BRING

- Suitable clothes for the time of year
- An OS map of the area
- Compass
- Notebook and pencil
- Mobile phone with camera or a camera
- Pair of secateurs for cutting bramble to allow access
- Water, flask, packed lunch
- Tree and plant identification books or suitable apps downloaded

Surveying

Each visit to your woodland will reveal more species as the seasons change and you become more focused on the diversity of species within it. However, many will have limits to their identification skills and how far they can go with guidebook identification, and there comes a point where asking for some professional help may become necessary.

Specialist help

There are specialist groups such as botanical societies, consisting of professional botanists who meet in different landscapes and record the distribution of wild plants in a particular area. I was fortunate to have a visit from the Sussex Botanical Recording Society to Prickly Nut Wood in my early days of management and it carried out an extensive survey of the woodland flora. A day spent with an enthusiastic group of knowledgeable botanists will open your eyes to the diversity of your woodland. Another option is to seek local knowledge. In most communities, there are usually individuals who have specialist knowledge in a particular field of flora or fauna – often more than happy to share their individual knowledge – and all of this will help build up a picture of your woodland's species. Gaining a good understanding of what species exist will help ensure that the management practices you undertake enhance rather than disturb the existing biodiversity.

Is your woodland ancient?

Ancient woodland indicator plants are a useful guide when trying to establish this (see pages 40–41). Due to their age, ancient woodlands often have fairly undisturbed soils and a range of plants that have developed over a long period of time within the particular environment the ancient woodland provides. There are a number of reasons why these plants indicate that a woodland is ancient – these include that most of these species cannot tolerate exposed conditions found outside woodlands and have relatively poor ability to colonize new sites.

More modern sites may have been established on land previously used for agriculture, meaning the soils may have been adapted by farming methods and are unsuitable for these species to thrive in. When you are surveying, these plant species being present gives stronger evidence for the site to be ancient.

LEFT: Spring is an important time for recording the diversity of ground flora in a broadleaf woodland.

BELOW: Epiphytic lichens can be used to help indicate ancient woodland.

Epiphytic lichens are another method botanists use to help identify the age of a woodland. In the 1970s, Dr Francis Rose concluded that lichens could also be used to identify ancient woodlands. On a personal note, the original moss, fern and lichen survey at Prickly Nut Wood was carried out by Francis Rose and Rod Stern and led to its designation as a Site of Special Scientific Interest (SSSI).

A selection of ancient woodland indicator plants are shown on pages 40–41. Larger lists and regional lists for the UK are available. Prickly Nut Wood contains over half the species listed in this table and a higher proportion are in the regional list. Along with historical documentation, lichens and other species present, it would be possible to deduce that Prickly Nut Wood was ancient woodland by these methods, had this work not already been undertaken.

Drawing up a plan

Time taken to survey and understand your woodland will enable you to make important decisions based on a good amount of research and information. The next stage will be to draw up a management plan for the woodland. For this you may decide to get help from a consultant or you may feel confident with your new knowledge of the woodland to draw up a plan. Templates are available through the Forestry Commission website and grants may well be available for drawing up the plan and towards future management. These grants change regularly and so for that reason, I have not listed what is currently available.

OTHER TYPES OF SURVEY

Butterfly, moth and bat surveys can be helpful and offer specialist knowledge. All species of bats are protected under law and most woodlands will have either resident or visiting bats. Bats can be detected with ultrasound detectors, and thermal-imaging cameras can be useful for identifying colonies in hollow trees.

Ancient woodland indicator species

This is a selection of ancient woodland indicator plants. The soil type of a particular ancient woodland and the density of the canopy will affect the species types that you might find.

Bilberry
Vaccinium myrtillus

Bitter vetch
Lathyrus linifolius

Bluebell *Hyacinthoides non-scripta*

Common cow-wheat
Melampyrum pratense

Dog's mercury
Mercurialis perennis

Early dog-violet
Viola reichenbachiana

Early purple orchid
Orchis mascula

Enchanter's nightshade
Circaea lutetiana

Giant fescue
Schedonorus giganteus

Goldilocks buttercup
Ranunculus auricomus

Great wood-rush
Luzula sylvatica

Hairy brome
Bromopsis ramose

Hairy wood-rush
Luzula pilosa

Hard fern
Blechnum spicant

Herb paris
Paris quadrifolia

Lily of the valley
Convallaria majalis

Moschatel
Adoxa moschatellina

Pendulous sedge
Carex pendula

Ramsons
Allium ursinium

Redcurrant
Ribes rubrum

Remote sedge
Carex remota

Sanicle
Sanicula europaea

Scaly male fern
Dryopteris affinis agg.

Slender St John's-wort
Hypericum pulchrum

Small-leaved lime
Tilia cordata

Spindle
Euonymus europaeus

Toothwort
Lathraea squamaria

Water avens
Geum rivale

Wild service tree
Sorbus torminalis

Wood anemone
Anemone nemorosa

Wood horsetail
Equisetum sylvaticum

Wood melick
Melica uniflora

Wood millet
Milium effusum

Wood sorrel
Oxalis acetosella

Woodruff
Galium odoratum

Wood sedge
Carex sylvatica

Wood speedwell
Veronica montana

Wood spurge
Euphorbia amygdaloides

Wych elm
Ulmus glabra

Yellow archangel
Lamiastrum galeobdolon

Yellow pimpernel
Lysimachia nemorum

Tree diseases

The increase in tree diseases across Great Britain is of great concern. I am not going to highlight the depressingly long list of diseases that are currently prevalent. Instead, I will look at the reasons for the increase of tree disease and what we can do to give our future woodlands the best chance of survival going forwards.

Climate change threat

As a forester, I monitor the risk to our native trees and there is no doubt that many tree species are under threat. This threat comes from many angles – climate change is producing fast-changing weather patterns that can cause stress to trees and the changes are happening at a pace where trees are not having a long time period to adapt as they might do to gradual change.

As our climate warms, some species will struggle to survive in the climatic zones they currently inhabit. For example, beech (*Fagus sylvatica*) is likely to struggle to survive in the south of England with increasing temperature. When a tree is growing in an environment where it is at the edge of its climatic comfort zone, the tree becomes stressed, opening up opportunities for diseases. An increase in monocultural plantings over the last century has also created an environment where, once disease establishes, it spreads easily from tree to tree and affects large areas of forest.

Biosecurity

Our biosecurity measures in Great Britain have been poor to say the least. As an island it is possible to have stringent controls in place when it comes to the importation of trees and plants but the relative ease of these arriving from the EU has allowed diseases to arrive. *Phytophera* is a plant pathogen that has many mutations and, in particular, *Phytophera ramorum* has caused widespread disease in larch trees in the UK, meaning thousands of acres of trees have had to be felled and, in many cases, destroyed. It has been traced back to imports of plants to UK garden centres from Belgium and Holland.

I remember visiting Australia in the 1980s and being impressed with their biosecurity measures. No food could be brought into the country, shoes had to be washed and no mud or soil on the soles could be imported. Before leaving the plane, we were all spray disinfected. Had we had such measures in place, the volume of tree diseases we are now dealing with in Great Britain could have been greatly reduced.

There is an interesting parallel comparison when we look at biosecurity and plant diseases and biosecurity and human diseases. Controlling spread of tree diseases once they are established in a country also needs improved biosecurity measures and, in particular, improved education. For the past ten years, I have been asking people who arrive at Prickly Nut Wood for a course or woodland visit to arrive with washed footwear for biosecurity reasons. When I explain to the group how easy it is to collect spores of plant pathogens on the soles of one's boots from a walk in the woods and then distribute them into a different wood on another walk, the reply is often 'I never thought of that'. A strong government educational campaign on plant disease biosecurity is well overdue. Contractors moving plants and vehicles from one woodland to another should wash down all wheels and tracks to reduce the risk of transfer of disease between woodlands.

Woodlander's story: diversifying sweet chestnut coppice

Much of Prickly Nut Wood is sweet chestnut coppice and there are about 42,000 acres (17,000ha) of similar woodland across south-east England. It grows vigorously, casts a heavy shade and few species can compete with it as the regrowth is too fast for most species growing from seed.

I have been experimenting with a second coppice cut four years after the previous long-rotation cut. This gives me coppice material but also allows naturally regenerating species such as birch and alder to take hold. These pioneer trees germinate when the light reaches the woodland floor after a long-rotation sweet-chestnut coppice cut. They are given extra light by the second coppice four years later. The birch and alder are then drawn up by the fast-growing stems of the sweet chestnut and a more diverse woodland structure begins.

My monocultural coppice of 100 per cent sweet chestnut has now evolved to 85 per cent with 15 per cent mixed broadleaf over a four-year period. These are small steps in encouraging more diversity. New species could also be planted after the first cut to further diversify the stand. The poorer the stocking rate of the initial sweet chestnut stand, the higher the percentage of mixed broadleaves will be achieved.

Diversifying a sweet chestnut coppice stand.

Another example of where we needed to be vigilant with biosecurity measures was the outbreak of Asian longhorn beetle in Paddock Wood, Kent, England, in 2012. The beetle, whose larvae cause devastating destruction to trees, is believed to have arrived when empty pallets were thrown out of a lorry into the woodland. The pallets originated in China and the eggs were already laid in the pallet timber. They hatched out and the beetles laid fresh eggs in trees, particularly sycamore. The outbreak was subject to rapid eradication action, and annual surveys since then have found no evidence of a continuing presence.

Biosecurity vigilance, using local rather than imported timber, choosing suitable species for climate change and diversifying our woodlands in species – whether new plantings or established woodland – are all measures we can take to help the growth and survival of future forests.

ABOVE: An Asian longhorn beetle.
OPPOSITE: A majestic beech on the edge of a ride at Prickly Nut Wood.

Pests

There are a number of pests you may come across, that affect the growing of trees in woodlands. Here, I highlight the most problematic ones, along with some options and ideas for controlling them.

Deer

Whether deer are a major pest to your woodland or not will vary geographically. Where I am based, in the south of England, the deer population is very high in numbers and the damage can be substantial to young trees or coppice regrowth. To give an indication of that increase, I can refer to my own observations over the past 30 years. Thirty years ago, I would see deer on average once every three weeks and they would be roe deer – now I see deer on average three times a day and they will be roe, fallow or muntjac. This increase has happened due to the large amount of woodland in the area I live and increased numbers of species escaped from deer farms and parks.

Species vary in their behaviour patterns – the roe tend to reside in and around the woodland area whereas the fallow form large herds and can travel quite a distance, causing a large amount of damage to tree crops in a very short period of time. Deer have every right to reside in woodlands but, with no natural predators, their numbers will soon get out of balance in the landscape and will need controlling.

Shooting deer

The shooting of deer in Great Britain is controlled by the Deer Act, which ensures any shooting of deer is carried out in the correct season for the particular species and those carrying out the shooting are properly qualified and licensed. Qualification involves obtaining a deer-stalking certificate and a class 1 firearms licence. The deer-stalking certificate involves marksmanship, field craft, identification and butchery. The firearms licence will need to be approved by the police.

With deer moving throughout the landscape, a coordinated regional approach for controlling numbers is the most successful management method. If you need to control deer within your woodland, you can engage a qualified stalker or contact the local forestry authority, which should be able to put you in touch with a local coordinator or deer stalker. The installation of high seats increases safety as shots are fired at a downward angle.

A portable ladder high seat soon blends into the woodland environment.

ABOVE: Native red squirrel.
ABOVE LEFT: Grey squirrel drey being lofted.

Grey Squirrels

In a recent survey by the Royal Forestry Society (RFS), grey squirrels came out top as the biggest threat facing woodland owners in Great Britain. I was surprised by this as I feel tree diseases to be far more threatening, but then at Prickly Nut Wood the grey squirrel population is currently under control. Grey squirrels are an introduced species that have thrived in Great Britain and have, through their larger size and the fact that they carry squirrelpox virus but don't suffer from it, driven the native red squirrel to become an endangered species.

The grey squirrel also causes severe damage to broadleaf trees. Areas where broadleaves are grown and the grey squirrel population is allowed to thrive, leave a woodland full of dying or poor-specimen trees of no commercial value. The grey squirrel strips the bark and inner bast for both materials to make its drey (nest) and for the sugars in the sap that provide food. This process often ring-barks the tree, causing a stop to the flow of sap and killing off the tree above where the grey squirrel has caused the damage. The grey squirrel will also eat bird's eggs and occasional fledglings from the nest. Grey squirrels have no natural predators, although pine martins in Scotland and northern England are known to predate on the grey squirrel.

Grey squirrel control methods

At Prickly Nut Wood, I control grey squirrel numbers through using lofting poles to remove the dreys, by shooting them with an air rifle and with the help of two squirrel-trained lurchers that 'point' to squirrels in the trees. This takes time and vigilance through the winter months but has proved a successful management programme in keeping the numbers in balance.

Traps can also be used to control grey squirrels and can be effective, but if you choose to use traps it is essential you regularly check them.

The latest Government-supported attempt to control the grey squirrel is to feed them an oral contraceptive. Although I can see the benefits of this plan in reducing grey squirrel numbers, and therefore benefitting the red squirrel, I am always concerned when, as humans, we tamper with nature to control pests. The effects of controlling rabbits with myxomatosis should be a cautious reminder of this. My concern with feeding oral contraceptives to grey squirrels is how to introduce the contraceptive to them without other similar species also being affected, but only time will tell.

Rabbits

Rabbits can cause significant damage to young trees and coppice regrowth, in particular to hazel coppice. I have seen the young regrowth of hazel coppice eaten to the ground by rabbits and, over time, the trees can eventually die. The Pests Act of 1954 declared England and Wales (with the exception of the City of London and the Isles of Scilly) a rabbit clearance area. This act not only allows the control of rabbits on farmland and woodland, it makes it the responsibility of the landowner to control them. There are many ways to control rabbits – shooting and trapping are well-used methods – but to get a population under control, ferreting of the rabbit warren over the winter prior to the breeding season will bring down numbers considerably and is the best starting point for controlling the population.

Plant pests

There are a number of plant pests that you could find in your woodland. Japanese knotweed (*Fallopia japonica*) is a controlled plant under the Wildlife and Countryside Act 1981 in the UK. If you have knotweed, I would suggest having it treated at the earliest opportunity. You cannot try to remove it and dispose of the plant as that could spread it to other areas and you will be liable if it spreads from your woodland to other land.

Rhododendron (*Rhododendron ponticum*) is now listed on schedule 9, part 2 of the Wildlife and Countryside Act 1981. This means it is a legal requirement to take due diligence to prevent the plant from spreading to the wild. For many woodlands, rhododendron is already established and in some areas it has taken over large parts of the landscape. In Snowdonia National Park, Wales, rhododendron has spread to over 4,900 acres (2,000ha). It is a tough plant to control and it is one where I would recommend careful herbicide application. The plants can be either injected or cut to the ground and the regrowth spot sprayed.

Rhododendron also acts as a host plant for the disease *Phytophera ramorum*, which can then spread to trees such as larch and sweet chestnut. I have cleared over 80 acres (32ha) of rhododendron at Prickly Nut Wood and surrounding woodland, but educating neighbours with rhododendron on their land is still a challenge. If you have even small amounts of rhododendron in your woodland, early removal is key to controlling its spread.

Other invasive plant species to look out for in woodlands are giant hogweed (*Heracleum mantegazzianum*) and Himalayan balsam (*Impatiens glandulifera*).

ABOVE:
Rhododendron
ponticum *bordering
Prickly Nut Wood.
More education is
needed to encourage
people to remove it
from their land.*

FAR LEFT:
Himalayan balsam.

*LEFT: Giant
hogweed.*

Legal requirements

Whether you are a woodland owner or just working in one, there are some key areas of legislation you will need to be aware of. Which insurance options you choose will depend on the woodland, and the activities you are carrying out there, but both owners and contractors will need public liability as a minimum.

Public and Employer's Liability Insurance

This type of insurance is essential cover for all woodland owners and contractors. There are many options depending on the level of cover you need, but for small woodland owners the Small Woods Association may be able to offer you the best deal. Signage is an important part of woodland insurance. Even if you are working in private woodland with no public access, warning signs should be used for those straying off the path.

If you employ anyone in your woods or engage volunteers working in the woods then you must have employer's liability insurance. This can be purchased as one insurance package with public and employer's liability grouped together.

Tool Insurance

There is a range of packages for insuring tools for contractors, whether the tools are at work or in transit in a vehicle. Leaving the tools in a locked shed overnight in the woods can prove more difficult but speak to your chosen provider. Many insurance providers that insure woodlands can tailor-make a package for your needs.

Chainsaw Training

Chainsaw training and assessment is provided by LANTRA or NPTC in the United Kingdom. You will need to have the correct qualification for the size of trees you are going to fell and will not find employment in woods without these qualifications. Woodland owners should not employ anyone on their land who does not have the correct qualifications. For the woodland owner who just wants to cross-cut firewood, suitable courses are available. A chainsaw is a dangerous tool in untrained hands – the courses focus on safety and I recommend everyone working with a chainsaw to attend one.

Legal Status of Land and Species

The legal status of land and species will vary depending upon the law of each country. These laws are regularly updated and, with the UK, changes are likely, so please check for the most recent information via Government websites.

There are a number of land designations used to conserve woodlands and particular habitats they contain. These, for example, could be National Nature Reserves, RAMSAR (wetland) sites, SPA (Special Protection Areas), or SSSI (sites of special scientific interest). Any designation should come up in a land search or by checking the Government mapping site (magic. defra.gov.uk). If you are managing woodland on one of these sites, permission for works will need to be granted and approval of a management plan for the site.

Endangered species are protected under the Conservation of Habitats and Species Regulations 2017 (as amended) and, from a woodland management perspective, all species of bats, dormice, great crested newts, otters, smooth snakes and sand lizards have the high level of protection previously covered by the European Habitats Directive. If these species are identified in your woodland – and most woodlands will contain bats – as a woodland owner, you are legally responsible for ensuring your management activities do not disturb their habitat. Best practice guidelines for England are available from the Forestry Commission and Natural England.

OPPOSITE: Wherever you are felling or carrying out forestry operations, signage should be used.

ABOVE: Prickly Nut Wood apprentices get to spend the winter felling coppice with me after they have passed their chainsaw course.

LEFT: Entrance to a badger sett.

FELLING LICENCES

Felling licences or felling permission will need to be obtained from your regional forestry department. In England, felling licences can be applied for to fell trees in a particular area of wood as an individual licence, or can be contained within a woodland management plan agreed with the Forestry Commission and contain felling approval for different compartments within a woodland over a number of years. If you are only felling a small amount of timber, for personal firewood, for example, you can do this without a felling licence, provided you do not fell more than 176.5 cubic feet (5 cubic metres) of timber in any quarter of a year.

Other examples of where you do not need a felling licence are:

- If you are felling trees of a diameter of less than 3in (8cm) overbark, measured just over 4ft (1.3m) from the ground.
- If you are thinning a woodland as part of a future timber crop, you can fell trees of 4in (10cm) or less overbark, measured 4ft (1.3m) from the ground.
- If you are felling coppice, you can fell trees of 6in (15cm) or less overbark, measured 4ft (1.3m) from the ground.
- If you are at all uncertain as to whether you need a licence or not, contact your regional forestry department. If you fell trees without a licence, you can be fined for illegal felling.

OPPOSITE: The forestry building
at Prickly Nut Wood is used
throughout the year.

*The forestry building being used by apprentices Ryan and Rachel
learning to make sweet chestnut gate hurdles.*

Tree Preservation Orders (TPOs)

TPOs are more commonly found on particular trees or small
areas of woodland, usually near human habitation. TPOs are
controlled by the local planning authority and you will need to
apply to them before carrying out any works on trees where a
TPO is present.

Planning Law

Please check your local region and government policy to get the
latest updates and position, as planning law is subject to review
and change.

Planning law and woodlands will depend on the law and
policy in individual countries. In England you are allowed to
stay overnight in your woodland for 28 days a year without
planning permission (also see Chapter 8, page 168 on camping).
The 28-day rule can work well for woodland owners who wish to
spend weekends in their woodland carrying out activities during
the day and enjoying a campfire and a night under the stars.

Seasonal stays

There is legislation in England that allows for seasonal forestry
workers to stay in a caravan for a particular season. The
definition and length of season is a grey area in planning law.
If, for example, you stayed in a woodland to make charcoal for
a three-month season and you could show that charcoal was an
important part of your business, you could stay as a seasonal
forestry worker for that period of time but would need to leave
the woodland once your season was finished.

Permanent stays

If you wish to live permanently in your woodland, you are
unlikely to get planning permission in England, unless
your woodland is of a size you can show that you can earn a
living from it. You will also need to show business figures
and projections as well as show an essential reason or
reasons why you need to live in the woodland rather than
local accommodation. You will at best be given a temporary
permission and then a period of time (usually three to five
years) to show the legitimacy of your forestry business
enterprise before having the option to apply for planning
permission for a dwelling.

Permitted buildings

Forestry buildings (barns), which have no residential element,
are a permitted development right for a woodland owner
running a forestry business. With permitted development
rights you will have to notify your local planning authority of
your attention to build a forestry building, its size, materials
and its position within the woodland.

In Scotland, the charity Reforesting Scotland has worked on
a project called the '1,000 Hut Project'. Planning permission
is needed but 'hutting' is now becoming accepted in the
planning system under the following definition: '*A hut: a simple
building used intermittently as recreational accommodation (i.e.
not a principal residence); having an internal floor area of no more
than 30m²; constructed from low-impact materials; generally not
connected to mains water, electricity or sewerage; and built in such
a way that it is removable with little or no trace at the end of its life.
Huts may be built singly or in groups.*'

Hutting offers the possibility for forest owners to establish a
hut or two in their forest and create a base from which to visit,
work and enjoy the woodland.

In Wales the 'one planet development' model gives woodland
owners and those with mixed woodland and agricultural land a
planning option to create a low-impact lifestyle working on the
land. Planning permission via this option currently offers the
best opportunity in the UK for living a low-impact sustainable
livelihood on the land.

ESTABLISHING NEW WOODLANDS

If you are fortunate enough to get the opportunity to plant a new woodland, there are a number of questions you should consider before you begin. This chapter aims to help you find the answers and to move forwards and enjoy planting and maintaining a new woodland.

Planning the planting scheme

Planting some trees is something everyone should try and achieve in their life. We all need to try and make a contribution towards climate change and our own ecological footprint, and planting a few trees will help. Planting a whole woodland will help a lot. Before you start, it is important to have a plan of how you are going to plant the woodland. How will it be maintained and what will it be used for when it is mature?

Long-term vision

I have planted woodlands for different purposes. One woodland was a long, narrow strip of land that I planted to be a wildlife corridor and shelterbelt, linking two established woodlands. This was planted with a mixed collection of native trees at an amenity spacing of about 800 trees per acre (2,000 trees per hectare), as timber production was not the priority for this woodland. The woodland is now mature and I enjoy watching the corridor in use. Long-tailed tits make their way through the corridor, seed feeding as they go, and I, too, feed on the bletted berries from the wild service trees.

I have planted woodlands where the plan has been for a firewood coppicing cycle with some long-term high-value timber as the woodland matures and a woodland where the end goal is to grow trees to old age where the local community can walk and enjoy the shady paths. So be clear what the wood will be used for and remember woodland life cycles are far longer than ours. The woodland will improve and mature over hundreds of years. Visit your potential woodland site and try to visualize the site as a woodland in 100 years' time – you will be leaving an important landscape for future generations.

What was the land used for previously?

Before planting a new woodland, it is important to analyse the soil and find out some past history of the land. Soil analysis will give you information on the pH of the soil and its nutrient levels. This will help you to make suitable species choices for the new woodland.

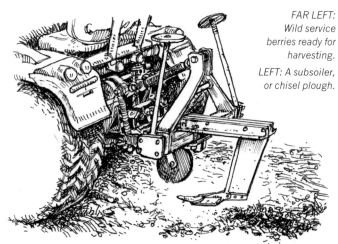

FAR LEFT: Wild service berries ready for harvesting.

LEFT: A subsoiler, or chisel plough.

My main advice here is choose species that want to grow in the soil conditions you have, rather than trying to change the soil to suit a particular tree species. Carry out soil analysis in a few different places across the site. You can purchase pH meters or basic soil testing kits and get a general idea, but you will need to send a soil sample away to a soil testing laboratory to get a more detailed analysis. If there is woodland adjacent to the site, look at the variety of tree and plant species. The presence of heather (*Calluna vulgaris*) and billberry (*Vaccinium myrtillus*) would give an indication of an acid soil whereas the presence of dogwood (*Cornus sanguinea*) and dog's mercury (*Mercurialis perennis*) would indicate a more alkaline soil.

If the land has been used for arable farming for a number of years, there is the possibility that a plough pan may have been formed. This is where the land has been ploughed at a similar depth for many years and the ground below that depth becomes compacted. This can make it harder for trees' roots to penetrate deep into the soil. This can be improved by using a subsoiler or chisel plough prior to planting.

A subsoiler breaks up the plough pan and prepares the soil for future planting. Try to chisel plough along the contours of the land as this will improve soil retention and drainage. Try to not plant the trees in the channels caused by the subsoiler as these can open up in the early years during dry summers.

CREATING SWALES IN THE LANDSCAPE

If the site is on a hillside where the rain run-off is fast, it may be worth considering digging 'swales' across the land. These are shallow ditches that are dug along the contour with the surplus soil banked up on the downhill side of the swale. In dry conditions, when there is summer rainfall, rather than see the rain run off quickly down the slope, it collects in the swale and then slowly absorbs into the soil below. Contour swales will be dug closer together on steeper hillsides to aid more water retention in the soil. I have found that the survival rate of young trees is greatly improved through the use of swales on a dry hillside. Over time the swale will begin to fill in with a build-up of leaf litter and twigs.

Natural regeneration

The simplest way to plant a woodland is to let nature do it for you. The landscape is naturally trying to turn into a woodland. If you remove livestock from a grass field, the grasses will grow long and seed, and other species will begin to colonize the sward. Over time, brambles will appear and then pioneer species such as birch will begin to colonize the land. Eventually it will evolve into a woodland. If the conditions are right, you can allow nature to create a woodland this way.

When deciding whether natural regeneration is a good option for your site, you should consider the availability of mother trees around the site. If the site is adjacent to another woodland or has mature hedgerows with standard trees that will produce seed (and provided they are species that would be suitable for your long-term vision of the woods), then fencing out rabbits and deer may be all you need to do to plant a woodland.

If you choose a good mast year then seed should be abundant. Trees will produce high volumes of seed after a dry summer. When there is a lack of water, trees become stressed and, in return,

trigger their own survival mechanism, which is to reproduce, resulting in the creation of a lot of seed. Fence your site after a dry summer and you are aiding your chances of getting a good volume of naturally regenerating trees.

Seeing a site evolve

Watching nature colonize farmed land and return it to woodland is an evolutionary process that can be a joy to observe. It will not take long before you will see a noticeable increase in wildlife, as the evolving woodland offers different habitats at its different stages of growth. Provided the stocking rates of naturally

regenerated trees are sufficient, it is possible in England to obtain a Forestry Commission grant for creating a woodland this way.

It will not be many years before you will need to consider some thinning and decide which trees to favour as the woodland evolves. Naturally regenerating beech or oak may need a little help by removing some of the faster-growing pioneers from close to them – this will ensure they have enough light to survive. The balance in thinning is important to ensure any target species such as oak are drawn up straight by the pioneer species around them.

Surrounded by woodland on three sides, this field has great potential to become a woodland through natural regeneration.

ABOVE: Birch is early to break into leaf, and here, the vibrant green of naturally regenerating birch is clear to see.

BELOW RIGHT: Naturally regenerating sweet chestnut in a clearing.

MIX IN SOME PLANTING

There is an opportunity to mix some planting into a naturally regenerating woodland. If your plan was to produce a high-value timber crop as part of your woodland vision, then planting the target species and thinning out the natural regeneration in favour of it could be a good silvicultural option. Remember to mark your target species when you plant them (I use a chestnut stake with a colour-painted top) as otherwise the target species can be hard to find amid a dense, naturally regenerating woodland.

Choices for planting a woodland

Direct seeding is one option for planting a woodland. This is carried out with a tractor and seed drill and can be an effective method for planting larger areas, especially where large seeds such as oak or sweet chestnut are being sown. Whether direct seeding or planting 'whips' (young seedling trees), you will need to carefully consider the source of any seed or whip you are going to plant.

Sourcing seed and whips

The first option is to collect or grow your own. For small-scale plantings, collecting local seed and either direct seeding or growing the seed on to whips and planting is a satisfying method of planting a woodland. However, you may be limited on species choice and certain trees needs different seed preparation to aid germination. Unless you are planning a small-scale tree nursery as part of your enterprise, it may be sensible to consider purchasing local nursery stock. In Great Britain, Forest Reproductive Regulations divide into four regions of provenance. By provenance, it refers to the region in which the trees were growing that produced the seed. These four regions of provenance are further subdivided into twenty-four native seed zones. This means that when buying whips from a nursery it is possible to know where the seed from the particular trees you are planting came from. Certain tree species have been improved through selective breeding programmes to help produce trees of better form for forestry purposes and if timber production is a key part of your woodland plans, then this may be a consideration in choosing your whips.

CONSIDERING CLIMATE CHANGE

For a long time, it has been considered that local provenance is the best choice for sourcing trees, as these trees will be adapted to the local climatic conditions and are known to grow well in that locality. However, climate change is making us reconsider this wisdom.

In Great Britain, the Forestry Commission now recommends that we choose seed from a latitude of two to five degrees south of where we are planting. This is based on considering a tree's life cycle and that a tree planted today will still be growing in one hundred years' time or more in different climatic conditions. I know of people choosing seed from five to ten degrees south as different climate projections show us different future scenarios. In south-east England, where I am a woodlander, it is predicted that dry summers and drought conditions will become increasingly common, putting trees at risk.

Choosing the correct source of nursery stock can be a difficult decision for you to make if you are planning a planting scheme for your woodland. My advice is to be diverse in your choices, both of latitude of seed choice and of species. Mixing a new planting of trees with some sourced from five degrees south, some from ten degrees south and some local provenance stock will help allow for different climate change scenarios.

Shagbark hickory.

Types of nursery stock

Nursery stock can be bareroot, cell grown or container grown. Cell-grown stock is often used to extend planting beyond the dormant winter period. When searching through a nursery catalogue, whether physical or online, the selection and choices can be daunting. Try to use a forestry nursery local to you that grows their own trees from seed, rather than imports trees and then sells them on. A local nursery may specialize in local provenance seed or may import seed from different latitudes and then grow that seed on into whips at the nursery.

Having decided the species and latitude of seed source, it will then be a choice of size of whip. For example, 12–20in (30–50cm) is a common size.

Don't be tempted to search for large trees to create an instant impact. The smaller whips will establish better, soon catch up or overtake larger trees and cost far less.

When to order and plant

The catalogue will then have information about how the trees have been grown in the nursery. This will look something like: '2 + 1' or '2 U 1'. The first number refers to the number of years the whip has been in the seedbed and the second number refers to the number of years it has been grown on since nursery intervention. The + refers to it being moved to a transplant bed and the U refers to having been undercut and grown on. Undercutting involves cutting the roots to promote the growth of more fibrous roots to help with establishment once planted. So, '2 + 1' means a three-year-old whip, two years spent in the seedbed and one year spent in a transplant bed.

Order your trees well in advance. Many nurseries sell out of forestry stock over the winter. Whips are often lifted bareroot and kept in a temperature-controlled environment until dispatch. They will then be dispatched (unless you are collecting) in plastic sacks to protect the roots from drying winds. Make sure you are ready to start planting when they arrive. If not, make sure you have a heeling-in area where the trees can be temporarily stored with their roots covered with soil to avoid any frosts. After March, bareroot stock becomes unavailable and cell-grown and container-grown trees become available.

Consider the local climatic conditions of where you are planting and avoid very frosty or windy days. My advice is to plan well; get the woodland planted with bareroot trees (if planting broadleaves) during the dormant winter period. For the UK, this is December to February and they will be in the ground and have the best opportunity of making a good start as the soil warms up.

LEFT: Most conifers establish quickly and it is not long before a field turns to forest.

OPPOSITE: Non-native conifers provide a lot of our timber needs. Growing them in continuous cover forestry systems rather than clearfell plantations is the best solution.

NATIVE OR NON-NATIVE?

There are certain woodlands (primarily ancient woodlands) where the native mixture of trees and plant species and associated biodiversity is so rich, I believe we should not plant any non-native species within them. However, climate change will affect these woodlands too, and over time their species mixture will evolve.

When it comes to planting new woodlands, we need to look towards the future. What trees will we need in 100 years' time? A balance of timber and food-producing trees? What trees will thrive in our changing climate? These questions must make us move away from non-native tree planting prejudices when it comes to new woodlands. Diversity for future uses, disease resilience and habitat creation will need to be the way forward.

Planting the woodland

If you have planned well, planting a woodland in the heart of winter can be a social occasion. Whether working as a team on a commercial planting or inviting friends and family to help, planting trees gives people the opportunity to connect with nature and feel empowered by doing something positive towards climate change. Not only that, it leaves a legacy for future generations.

By now, you will have decided on your planting distances and number of trees. I use a wooden grid made from roofing baton to be accurate with my planting distances. Don't worry if this all seems very uniform – as the woodland establishes and thinning takes place, the grid lines will soon break up. You will have thought through your extraction rides and where any timber in the future may exit the woodland site, and what protection measures you are using to keep the trees from browsing animals once they are planted.

ABOVE: Young oaks establishing in tree shelters; note one of the shelters needs re-staking or the tree will grow with an angled stem at the base.

PLANNING DIARY FOR YOUR WOODLAND

January	Design your woodland, choose species
April	Order trees for the following winter
May	Chisel plough if necessary
July/August	Order tree shelters, mulch mats, stakes (if using)
September	Prepare land (if a field, it may need topping)
October	Carry out any fencing
December–February	Plant woodland

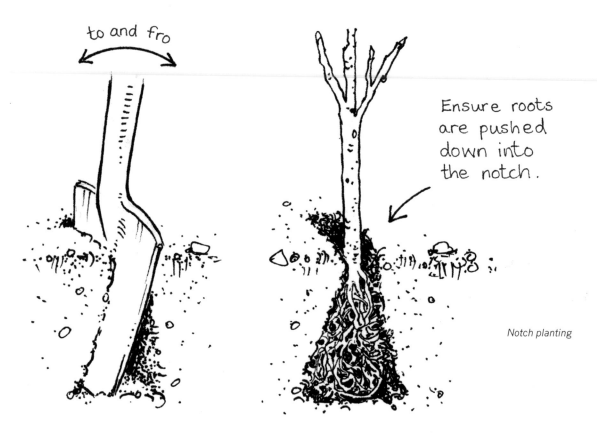

to and fro

Ensure roots are pushed down into the notch.

Notch planting

Type of planting system

Prior to planting, you will have worked out a system for the different species you are planting. You may be planting randomly, which can be fine, or you may have a particular planting plan for clumps of single species or a nurse cropping system. Nurse cropping involves planting in rows, often using a fast-growing (often coniferous) species as the nurse and the target crop in rows between the nurse crop. The nurse crop grows fast and creates shade on the trunk of the target species – this encourages the target species to grow straight and without many side branches. At the appropriate time, the nurse crop is removed, allowing the target species to grow to maturity. An example of this would be a target species of beech and a nurse crop of Lawson's cypress.

You will need to decide on the type of planting spades you are using and have enough spades for any helpers who will be planting with you. You will need to ensure that everyone has a bag of trees,

with the roots protected from the wind. Professional planting bags are available with a backpack-style harness, with multiple bags for mixed plantings. These should be considered if you are planning on planting multiple woodlands.

Instruction should be given to any helpers on planting techniques. If you

Planting backpack

are notch planting bareroot trees, ensure the notch is deep enough for the roots and well firmed up afterwards to close up the notch. Make sure to explain clearly the importance of protecting bare root trees from the wind. The tree should come out of the bag and into the notch in one quick movement. I have visited volunteer tree planting schemes where I see the bare root trees lying open to the elements on the ground prior to planting. Wind burns the root hairs and causes more losses to trees at planting time than anything else. Keep the roots out of the fresh air and your tree survival rate will be greatly enhanced.

Weed control

Another consideration will be whether to mulch the young trees. If planting into cultivated ex-arable land, it may not be necessary at the time of planting and aftercare weed control may be more relevant, but if planting into established pasture, it will be. Most commercial planting into pasture is done by spraying

What he had forgotten was that there was a thousand young fir trees to be planted in a neighboring spot which had been cleared by the woodcutters, and that he had arranged to plant them with his own hands. He had a marvellous power of making trees grow. Although he would seem to shovel in the earth quite carelessly, there was a sort of sympathy between himself and the fir, oak or beech that he was operating on, so that the roots took hold of the soil in a few days. When, on the other hand, any of the journeymen planted, although they seemed to go through an identically similar process, one quarter of the trees would die away during the ensuing August.

From *The Woodlanders* by Thomas Hardy

each planting area with a herbicide. This will leave marked brown patches in the pasture of where the tree is to be planted and will remove competitive plants and grasses from around the whip. This will be even more important if planting cell-grown trees, which are younger and smaller than whips and could be easily outcompeted by the growing vegetation.

Herbicide is by far the cheapest option per tree but if, like myself, you prefer to limit herbicide use, then the best alternative is mulching. Purpose-made mulch mats can be bought – these are made from a variety of different materials and will need to be pegged down. These can be made from recycling horticultural matting or any dark covering like carpet that will supress weed growth. When looking for recycled alternatives, consider what you are bringing into your new woodland – there will need to be a lot of material to mulch a new planting and it will need to be biodegradable. Purpose-made biodegradable hemp mulch mats and

mixed recycled organic fibre mats are now available individually or in a roll and these, although expensive, are a good solution.

If using a mulch mat it is important to fix them down firmly – loose mulch mats provide good homes for voles, which enjoy eating the young tree roots they find beneath the mats. Whatever method

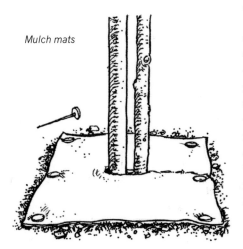

Mulch mats

you choose, the area around each tree to be weed controlled will need to be about 3 square feet (1 square metre).

If you have access to a woodchipper, then woodchip can be used as a mulch. The chip is best left in piles to partly compost prior to spreading around the trees. If using partially composted woodchip, I would recommend skimming off the turf prior to planting each tree and covering the bare soil with 4in (10cm) of woodchip mulch after planting.

If you know a local tree surgeon, it is worth finding out what they do with their woodchip. Many tree surgeons struggle to get rid of the chip and if you have a field that you are planning to plant as a woodland, offering them the opportunity to offload their woodchip in the field may, over time, give you a very cost-effective mulch solution. Do check that the woodchip has not come from diseased trees as that should not be introduced to a new woodland planting.

Protection and maintenance

Protecting young trees at planting time and in their early years is essential to ensuring your new woodland establishes well. The choices are whether to fence the new woodland site or use protective guards (tree shelters) on individual trees.

Badger gate in use.

The shape of the woodland will have an impact on the cost effectiveness of whether to fence. If the woodland is long and narrow, the length of fence needed could be a large capital outlay and it may be better to use individual tree shelters. However, if the new woodland site is less linear in shape, then fencing is likely to be the best option. A well-constructed fence will also help if your management strategy involves coppicing as the fence will be there to protect the regrowth after cutting.

Before choosing your choice of protection you need to establish the species you are planning to keep out. Deer in most parts of Great Britain are increasing in numbers and can destroy a planting of young trees in a short period of time. There is now a variety of deer species in Great Britain, from large species like red and fallow to the small

muntjac deer. So the size and design of fence must reflect the species that are present. Be aware that some species of deer such as fallow will roam in herds over large areas and just because you haven't seen them today, doesn't mean they won't be grazing on your young trees tomorrow!

Matching fencing to the species

There are a number of fencing designs available. Steel deer netting can be purchased by the roll and is typical of stock fencing, with the wires closer together at the bottom and getting further apart towards the top. The deer fence will need to be 6ft (1.8m) high for the larger species. Muntjac deer are very good at getting under fences, so in most cases it would be advisable to attach hexagonal wire rabbit netting to

the bottom section of the fence. This will also fence out rabbits but the wire mesh should be turned out 6in (15cm) towards the direction the rabbits would try to enter. This folded piece of fence should either be dug in, pegged down or weighed down with turf.

Rabbits will come to the edge of the fence and try to dig down at that point, so the folded fence works as a good

Post straining with strut.
Post straining box section.

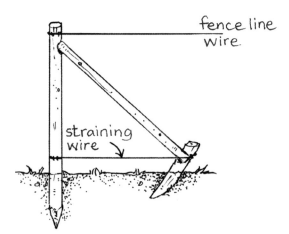

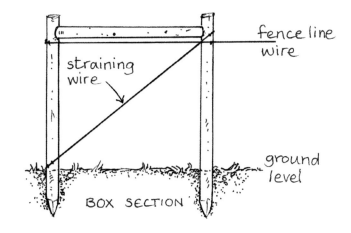

deterrent. Make sure there are no rabbit warrens inside the new woodland area – you would not want to fence them in! Ferreting any active warrens the previous winter before fencing would be advisable. If you have badgers on or near the site, they may have established runs through where you are planning to fence. Badgers do not like to be rerouted and will tear a hole through a mesh fence, so construct badger gates where the fence crosses their runs. Badger gates are like a large heavy duty cat flap and should be made from timber and be heavy to push open. Lightweight gates offer opportunities for rabbits.

Fence posts

You will need straining posts and struts for the fence posts – these are fitted where there is a change of direction in the fence or where a gate is to be positioned. Between the straining posts will be intermediate posts. For a 6ft (1.8m) deer fence, you will need straining posts of 6–7in (15–17.5cm) diameter and 9ft (2.8m) in length, with intermediate posts of 4in (10cm) diameter and 8ft (2.45m) in length. The intermediate posts should be less than 30ft (9m) apart.

When choosing fence posts, sweet chestnut has to be the first choice, for its durability and the knowledge that it has come from a sustainably managed coppice woodland. Deer fencing of this nature is no small undertaking and if you have limited experience of fencing, you should consider employing a local fencing contractor to carry out the work. They will be used to erecting deer fences and dealing with the challenges of undulating land – and they will have the necessary equipment and expertise to carry out the task.

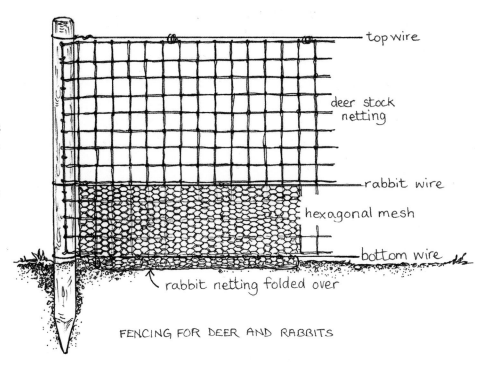

top wire

deer stock netting

rabbit wire

hexagonal mesh

bottom wire

rabbit netting folded over

FENCING FOR DEER AND RABBITS

ABOVE: Steel fence pattern for all deer and rabbits.
BELOW: Badger gate specification.

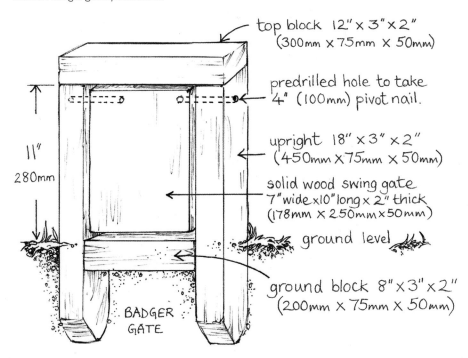

top block 12" x 3" x 2" (300mm x 75mm X 50mm)

predrilled hole to take 4" (100mm) pivot nail.

upright 18" x 3" x 2" (450mm x 75mm x 50mm)

solid wood swing gate 7" wide x 10" long x 2" thick (178mm x 250mm x 50mm)

ground level

ground block 8" x 3" x 2" (200mm x 75mm x 50mm)

11" 280mm

BADGER GATE

Types of fencing

Other fencing options for deer are rolls of plastic netting. These are usually used as temporary fences around freshly cut coppice and last long enough to allow the regrowth to get above browsing height. They are made of plastic and this often gets left in the woodland and not removed. In Scotland they are sometimes attached to a steel fence to make the fence more visible to capercaillie and black grouse, as there have been cases of injured birds flying into the steel mesh. Chestnut paling is also sometimes attached to create a clearer visible barrier for the birds.

Electric fencing is worth considering provided you are going to visit regularly and maintain it. There are solar- and wind-powered options available to help keep the fence charged but as grasses and plants grow and touch the fence it will short out, so control of competing vegetation is essential for its effectiveness.

Wooden fencing is an attractive, sustainable but more expensive option. Chestnut paling can be purchased in 6ft (1.8m) rolls and this makes a very good visual barrier. I have been using a chestnut post-and-rail deer fence around my vegetable garden with 6ft (1.8m) pales and this has proved successful in keeping out fallow, roe and muntjac deer.

Tree shelters

If you are not fencing then using tree shelters will be your other alternative. These are made from biodegradable plastic. However, in my experience by the time the new tree canopy closes over and the shelters are receiving little sunlight, they are still a long way from biodegrading. So expect that you will have to return at some point and remove them from the trees. I have successfully reused shelters by cutting them down their length and then re-securing them with string for a second use. If you can plant two woodlands with the same shelters, then the initial outlay becomes more cost effective.

Tree shelters come in different heights – taller to protect from larger species of deer – and they come as either a solid shelter or as a mesh. The solid shelters not only protect but act as a micro-greenhouse, creating a warm microclimate and for some species this gets the trees off to a vigorous start.

Wild cherry (*Prunus avium*) and small-leaved lime (*Tilia cordata*) are two species that I have had very good results with growing in tree shelters. Tree shelters need to be well staked. I use chestnut pales and hammer them securely into the ground before attaching the shelter. The shelters often have reusable cable ties to secure them to the stake. If they are not well staked and get blown from their vertical position in the wind, the tree will grow to the shape of the shelter and any hope of getting good-quality timber from the trees will be lost. Regular maintenance is essential.

OPPOSITE: A young woodland establishing with the aid of tree shelters.

LEFT: A steel deer fence. They need regular inspection, especially after high winds.

With the tree shelters removed, this broadleaf woodland has a closing canopy and is establishing well.

Planting in an existing woodland

Whether restocking after felling, adapting species or filling in after storm damage, planting in an existing woodland will often be most cost effective using tree shelters. The first thing to consider is how much light is getting to the woodland floor. If it is a small clearing within the woodland, it may be necessary to fell a few more trees to open up the canopy further and extend the amount of light entering the clearing before replanting. With small clearings it is advisable to choose shade-tolerant species to allow for restricted light as they establish.

Aftercare

Regular maintenance will help give your woodland the best start. If you have fencing around your trees, walk regularly around the fence to check for any damage or signs of animals getting in. If you have used tree shelters, check the stakes and cable ties are secure and that the shelter is upright. Always visit after high winds and check for any losses. It is not unusual to lose a few trees in the first year. These should be marked and replaced the following winter. Check for weed competition – a well-mulched tree will get off to a far better start than one that is competing with other plant species.

Enjoy the experience of your woodland growing – you are leaving an important landscape for future generations. The years will soon pass and you will no longer be looking down at whips but looking up at the closing canopy of the woodland above you.

SHADE-TOLERANT TREE SPECIES

Beech	*Fagus sylvatica*
Coast redwood	*Sequoia sempervirens*
Field maple	*Acer campestre*
Hornbeam	*Carpinus betulus*
Lawson's cypress	*Chamaecyparis lawsoniana*
Silver fir	*Abies alba*
Small-leaved lime	*Tilia cordata*
Sycamore	*Acer pseudoplatanus*
Western red cedar	*Thuja plicata*
Yew	*Taxus baccata*

Woodlander's story: planting my first woodland

I planted my first woodland 30 years ago. The work began the previous winter, when I coppiced some sweet chestnut and cleaved out 3,500 pales to support the tree shelters I was using. The land was on a hillside and had been a grass pasture for the past 20 years, so I was not worried about a plough pan, but the rainwater run-off was fast and so I decided to dig swales to allow slower water release into the soil on the slope. I used a water level to establish the contour and dug the swales about 3ft (90cm) wide and 1ft (30cm) deep. I dug three of them across the contour about 100ft (30m) apart and levelled out the dug soil on the slope below each swale.

I worked out my access routes for future extraction using the contours. The woodland was primarily for biodiversity, consisting of 11 native species with the target species for timber being wild cherry (*Prunus avium*) and wild service (*Sorbus torminalis*). I then hammered in the stakes for the shelters, marking the stakes for appropriate tree species. The trees arrived bareroot in early December and I heeled them into a small fenced-off enclosure I had prepared for their arrival.

Planting was soon underway – it was a good winter, crisp and bright and I made good progress with the planting, mainly working alone with my visions of the landscape I was transforming but occasionally with friends who would turn up for the day and bring laughter to the process.

Each tree was notch planted. I would scrape off the turf and then push the spade deep into the soil and move it back and forth, opening up a slit in the ground. My chosen tree would come out of the planting bag and straight into the ground, minimizing any wind that could scorch the roots. I would then firm up the slit and slide the tree shelter over the top and secure the cable ties to the chestnut stake. Each tree then had a mulch mat, pegged to the ground to give it the best possible chance. Within a few weeks it was all planted. At the time I looked out across a sea of tree shelters. Thirty years on, I am looking up into the canopy of a woodland.

Standing next to a wild cherry that I planted as a whip 30 years ago.

Tree species choice for new plantings

TREE SPECIES	BOTANICAL NAME	SOIL PREFERENCE	NATIVE SPECIES	BROADLEAF OR CONIFER
Alder, buckthorn	*Frangula alnus*	Neutral to acid	Native	Broadleaf
Alder, common	*Alnus glutinosa*	Wet, most soils	Native	Broadleaf
Alder, grey	*Alnus incana*	Neutral, most soils	Non-native	Broadleaf
Ash	*Fraxinus excelsior*	Neutral to alkaline	Native	Broadleaf
Aspen	*Populus tremula*	Damp, neutral to acid	Native	Broadleaf
Beech	*Fagus sylvatica*	Neutral to alkaline	Native	Broadleaf
Birch, downy	*Betula pubescens*	Tolerates most soils	Native	Broadleaf
Birch, silver	*Betula pendula*	Tolerates most soils	Native	Broadleaf
Blackthorn	*Prunus spinosa*	Tolerates most soils	Native	Broadleaf
Black locust	*Robinia pseudoacacia*	Prefers light soils	Non-native	Broadleaf
Black walnut	*Juglans nigra*	Neutral sandy loam	Non-native	Broadleaf
Box	*Buxus sempervirens*	Alkaline	Native (south GB)	Broadleaf evergreen
Cedar, western red	*Thuja plicata*	Tolerates most soils	Non-native	Conifer
Cherry, bird	*Prunus padus*	Neutral to alkaline	Native	Broadleaf
Cherry, wild	*Prunus avium*	Tolerates most soils	Native	Broadleaf
Chestnut, sweet	*Castanea sativa*	Neutral to acid	Honorary native	Broadleaf
Crab apple	*Malus sylvestris*	Tolerates most soils	Native	Broadleaf
Cypress, Lawson's	*Chamaecyparis lawsoniana*	Tolerates most soils	Non-native	Conifer
Cypress, swamp	*Taxodium distichum*	Tolerant, wet soils	Non-native	Conifer deciduous
Dogwood	*Cornus sanguinea*	Alkaline, damp	Native	Broadleaf
Elder	*Sambuscus nigra*	Tolerates most soils	Native	Broadleaf
Elm, English	*Ulmus procera*	Tolerates most soils	Native (south GB)	Broadleaf
Elm, wych	*Ulmus glabra*	Tolerant, heavy soils	Native	Broadleaf
Fir, Douglas	*Pseudotsuga menziesii*	Neutral to acid	Non-native	Conifer
Fir, silver	*Abies alba*	Tolerates most soils	Non-native	Conifer
Guelder rose	*Viburnum opulus*	Neutral soils	Native	Broadleaf

SILVICULTURAL MANAGEMENT	TIMBER USES	DURABILITY	OTHER COMMENTS
Coppice, lower tree layer	Charcoal	Non-durable	Butterfly food
Coppice	Charcoal, craft use	Non-durable	Nitrogen fixing, dye
Suckers, nurse crop	Charcoal, craft use	Non-durable	Nitrogen fixing, windbreak
Coppice, high forest	Multiple craft uses	Non-durable	Chalara die-back, do not plant
Suckers, high forest	Pulpwood	Non-durable	May become dominant
High forest, pollard	Saw log, furniture	Non-durable	Shade tolerant
Coppice, pioneer species	Firewood, craftwork, pulp	Non-durable	Damper soils than silver birch
Coppice, pioneer species	Firewood, craftwork, pulp	Non-durable	Likes light, sandy soils
Suckers, underwood	Walking sticks, mauls	Moderate durability	Sloes, butterflies and moths
Suckers, high forest	Construction, saw log	Very durable	Nitrogen fixing
High forest	Saw logs, furniture	Very durable	Nuts, high-value timber
Underwood, coppice	Tool handles, carving	Durable	Good for bees
High forest, continuous cover	Cladding, shingles	Very durable	Bast used for weaving
Coppice	Turnery	Moderatly durable	Good for bees
Suckers, high forest	Turnery, furniture, saw log	Durable	Good for bees
Coppice, high forest	Multiple craft uses, fencing	Very durable	Nuts
Coppice	Firewood, mauls	Non-durable	Fruit
High forest, continuous cover	Construction, cladding	Durable to very durable	Avoid waterlogged soil
Coppice, high forest	Construction	Durable to very durable	Likes wet woodland sites
Coppice	Artists' charcoal, craftwork	Non-durable	Good for wildlife
Coppice	Craftwork, whistles, pipes	Non-durable	Grown for flowers and berries
Suckers, high forest	Furniture, saw logs	Non-durable	Disease-resistant trees available
Coppice	Saw logs, craftwork	Non-durable	Bast used for seat weaving
High forest	Saw logs, construction	Moderately durable	Very stable timber
High forest, continuous cover	Saw logs, plywood, paper	Non-durable	Resin, used for turpentine
Coppice, lower tree layer	Skewers	Non-durable	Medicinal bark, good for birds

Tree species choice for new plantings cont.

TREE SPECIES	BOTANICAL NAME	SOIL PREFERENCE	NATIVE SPECIES	BROADLEAF OR CONIFER
Hawthorn	*Crataegus monogyna*	Tolerates most soils	Native	Broadleaf
Hazel	*Corylus avellana*	Tolerates most soils	Native	Broadleaf
Hickory, shagbark	*Carya ovata*	Neutral to acid, damp	Non-native	Broadleaf
Holly	*Ilex aquifolium*	Tolerates most soils	Native	Broadleaf evergreen
Hornbeam	*Carpinus betulus*	Tolerant, heavy soils	Native	Broadleaf
Juniper	*Juniperus communis*	Neutral to alkaline	Native	Conifer
Larch, European	*Larix decidua*	Neutral to acid, damp	Non-native	Conifer deciduous
Lime, small-leaved	*Tilia cordata*	Tolerates most soils	Native (south GB)	Broadleaf
Maple, field	*Acer campestre*	Tolerant, heavy soils	Native	Broadleaf
Maple, Norway	*Acer platanoides*	Tolerates most soils	Non-native	Broadleaf
Monkey puzzle	*Araucaria araucana*	Tolerates most soils	Non-native	Conifer
Oak, English	*Quercus robur*	Tolerates most soils	Native	Broadleaf
Oak, sessile	*Quercus petraea*	Tolerant, moist	Native	Broadleaf
Pine, lodgepole	*Pinus contorta*	Tolerant of poor soils	Non-native	Conifer
Pine, maritime	*Pinus pinaster*	Neutral to acid soils	Non-native	Conifer deciduous
Pine, Scots	*Pinus sylvestris*	Tolerant, well-drained	Native	Conifer
Poplar, aspen	*Populus tremula*	Tolerant, avoid sandy	Native	Broadleaf
Redwood, coast	*Sequoia sempervirens*	Tolerant, avoid sandy	Non-native	Conifer
Rowan	*Sorbus aucuparia*	Neutral to acid	Native	Broadleaf
Spindle	*Euonymus europaeus*	Neutral to alkaline	Native	Broadleaf
Sycamore	*Acer pseudoplatanus*	Tolerates most soils	Non-native	Broadleaf
Whitebeam	*Sorbus aria*	Neutral to alkaline	Native	Broadleaf
Wild service tree	*Sorbus torminalis*	Neutral to acid	Native	Broadleaf
Willow, almond	*Salix triandra*	Tolerant, wet soils	Native (south GB)	Broadleaf
Willow, goat	*Salix caprea*	Tolerant, wet soils	Native	Broadleaf
Willow, osier	*Salix viminalis*	Tolerant, wet soils	Native	Broadleaf
Yew	*Taxus baccata*	Neutral to alkaline	Native	Conifer

SILVICULTURAL MANAGEMENT	TIMBER USES	DURABILITY	OTHER COMMENTS
Coppice	Turnery, carving, firewood	Durable	Good bee tree
Coppice	Multiple craft uses	Non-durable	Nuts
Coppice, high forest	Tool handles, craftwork, saw logs	Non-durable	Nuts, very hard dense wood
Coppice	Turnery, firewood	Non-durable	Good for birds
Coppice	Floorboards, turnery, charcoal	Non-durable	Traditionally used for cogs
Lower tree layer	Carving	Durable	Medicinal oil, flavouring gin
High forest, continuous cover	Construction, saw logs	Durable	Resin
Coppice, high forest	Turnery, carving, saw logs	Non-durable	Edible leaves, weavable bast
Coppice	Turnery, furniture, carving	Non-durable	Can be grown on into a saw log
High forest, continuous cover	Saw logs, veneer, carving	Non-durable	Ash alternative in south-east GB
High forest	Saw logs, construction	Non-durable	Produces high volume of nuts
High forest	Saw logs, construction, firewood	Very durable	Often a standard with coppice
High forest	Saw logs, construction, firewood	Very durable	Found in ancient woodlands
High forest, nurse tree	Construction, poles	Moderately durable	Good for poor upland soils
High forest	Construction, poles, saw logs	Moderately durable	Good for coastal planting
High forest	Construction, poles, saw logs	Moderately durable	Scottish ancient woods
High forest, suckers	Pallets, matches	Non-durable	Slow-burning wood
High forest, coppice	Construction, fencing, saw logs	Durable	Best in SW England and Wales
Coppice	Carving, furniture	Non-durable	Berries for birds
Lower tree layer	Skewers, artists' charcoal	Non-durable	Important for wildlife
High forest, coppice	Saw logs, veneer, carving	Non-durable	Ash alternative in northern GB
Coppice	Turnery, firewood	Non-durable	Berries for birds
High forest, suckers	Furniture, joinery, firewood	Non-durable	Bletted berries good to eat
Coppice	Basketry, spars, wattle, charcoal	Non-durable	Mainly in south-east England
Coppice	Carving, firewood	Non-durable	Important early pollen for bees
Coppice	Basketry, spars, wattle, charcoal	Non-durable	Often used on degraded lands
High forest	Furniture, carving	Very durable	Culturally important

SILVICULTURAL MANAGEMENT

This chapter will look at the techniques and practices of different woodland management systems. A woodland might have just one type of management or it may contain a number of different practices in different areas of the woodland.

Coppicing

Coppicing is a unique form of woodland management that can be seen as both managing for timber and managing for wildlife and increasing biodiversity. It is also culturally important in our woodland heritage.

Coppicing is often low impact with areas of on-cycle hazel coppice managed purely by hand tools. The resulting cut poles are small enough to be carried out of the woodland by hand. The cut area allows the light to reach the woodland floor and in turn stimulates dormant wildflowers to appear, as well as butterflies that feed from them.

The key with any coppice management is to have a cutting cycle, so that you are always cutting an area of coppice every year. This way you create a patchwork throughout the woodland of coppice with different ages of growth. This ensures you have an annual supply of material for craftwork or firewood and in turn there is always a newly cut area for the light to reach the woodland floor and areas of different ages of regrowth for the associated bird species that have a preference for that habitat.

Cutting on-cycle hazel coppice

With on-cycle hazel this will usually be coppice that has been cut every six to eight years. Areas are usually defined by natural boundaries such as streams or woodland rides but if not are often defined by 'cant' markers. These are stems of coppice that have been cut higher than the rest of the coppice to stand out as markers. Where possible, try to cut to the original 'cant' markers as this is the way the woodland has been cut previously. Before you begin, ensure you have the necessary equipment and have allowed enough time for the coppicing. Estimate how long you think it will take and then add on 25 per cent.

Unless you have a lot of experience with cutting coppice you are likely to underestimate the time involved.

Coppicing is a winter activity and the trees should be cut during the dormant winter period. Being organized as you cut the coppice is key to efficiently working the cant. The coppice can be cut with a billhook, pruning saw, bow saw or chainsaw (see Chapter 5 for more on tool use). Cutting with a billhook takes a lot of practice to get the cut low enough and not to chop down on the stem, which can leave a rough finish. A bow saw is good but can be difficult to get between the rods; a pruning saw is ideal as it is small, light and gets between the rods. A chainsaw is fast. I use a battery chainsaw with

a carving bar. This is quiet, quick and gets between the rods. The batteries are charged by solar power.

The coppice stool should be cut as close as possible to the ground – this ensures the next cycle of regrowth will be straight and true. Try to cut each stem with a slight slope away from the centre of the stool. As you cut each stool, lay the cut material in long drifts to the side of the stool you have been cutting. All the material should be laid in the drift facing the same way, so that when you start to 'work up' the drift, the cut rods are easy to pick up and not tangled.

Freshly cut hazel coppice in late January, Tegleys Wood, Hampshire.

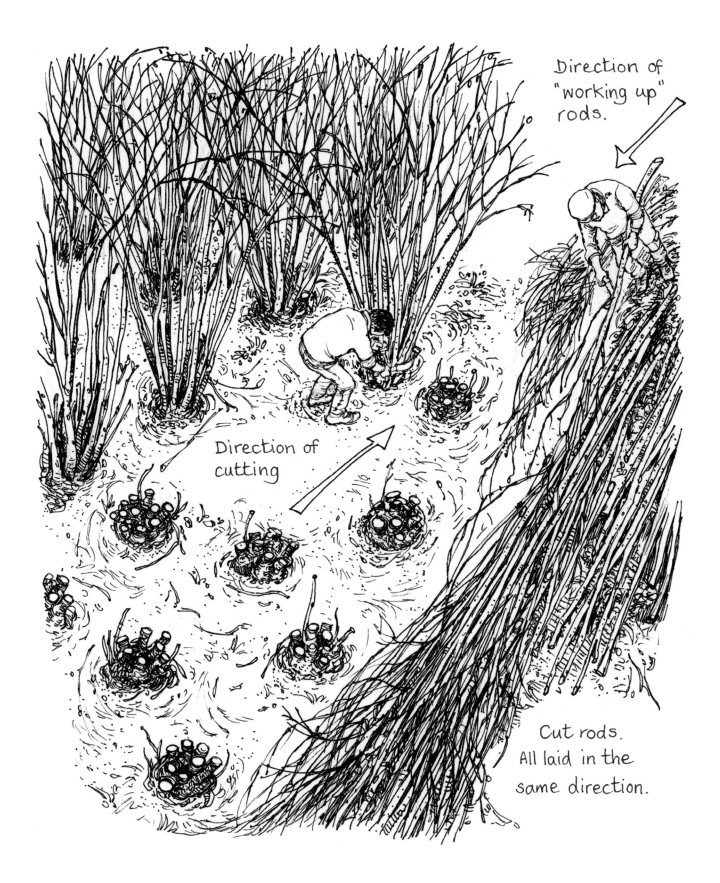

Direction of "working up" rods.

Direction of cutting

Cut rods. All laid in the same direction.

Hazel laid in drifts and being 'worked up' with a billhook.

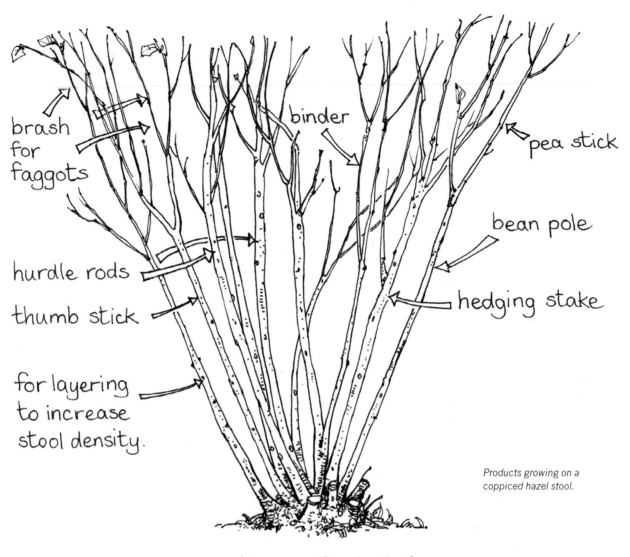

brash for faggots

binder

pea stick

hurdle rods

thumb stick

for layering to increase stool density.

bean pole

hedging stake

Products growing on a coppiced hazel stool.

HAZEL PRODUCTS

Sorting the rods

Once you have cut enough material to make a couple of drifts, it is time to 'work up' or 'dress out' the rods. This involves snedding the rods by working with a billhook from the base of the rod towards the top, removing the small side branches as you go. At this stage you should know what products you are looking for from the copse and should be placing the snedded rods into product piles. If you are making hurdles, rods will be sorted into zales, weavers and cleavers. If you are looking for hedge-laying material, you will have product piles for stakes and binders (etherings).

Uses for brash

You will end up with a pile of brash from all the side branches and tops (lop and top). If the coppice is good quality you won't have too much of this and it will be mainly used for keeping your kettle boiling. If the coppice is poor quality then you will end up with a lot of brash and you might consider making brash faggots. These are used in river revetment work by the Environment Agency in Great Britain. (Details for making brash faggots can be found in my book *Woodland Craft*).

Other uses for brash will be pea sticks – these are fan-shaped brash from the top of a coppice rod, usually cut to between 5 to 7 ft (150 to 210cm). Often, the main part of the rod can be cut for a beanpole with a pea stick made from the top. These products are sold to allotment groups and garden centres and usually appear at the beginning of April. Once cut, hazel coppice is one of the best coppice habitats for wildflowers. The regular short cycles enable the build-up of a diverse ground flora. Hampshire and Dorset are home to some of the finest hazel copses in Great Britain.

Layering

Cranbourne Chase and Kings Sombourne in Dorset and Hampshire are areas where the copse is so good, the cutting rights are carefully guarded. A top-quality, on-cycle hazel coppice will produce three times the product that a poorer-quality copse will produce. The quality can be improved by layering some of the stems each cycle. Look where there are gaps in the copse and layer into those gaps. I usually layer about 6 ft (1.8m) away from an existing stool. Layering involves increasing the stocking rate of the copse. This will produce a higher volume of straighter rods. This is done by leaving a rod on the outside and uphill side (if on a slope) of the stool when you are cutting.

Once you have finished working that area and before the rod has broken into leaf, the rod can be bent over and part of it pegged into the ground using a fork of hazel. Where the rod makes contact with the soil, I remove a small piece of bark on the underside of the hazel rod with a knife. I dig away a little soil at the point where the rod will be pegged down and, having hammered the peg into the ground, I then cover it over with soil. The top of the rod can be further supported by a smaller fork to ensure the sap will flow to it. Sap only flows uphill, hence not layering downhill on a slope. The rod will take root where it is pegged into the ground and, after a couple of years, it can be severed from the mother tree. The final part of ensuring your copse will grow well is protecting it from predators. This will usually involve temporary or permanent fencing or very vigilant deer stalking.

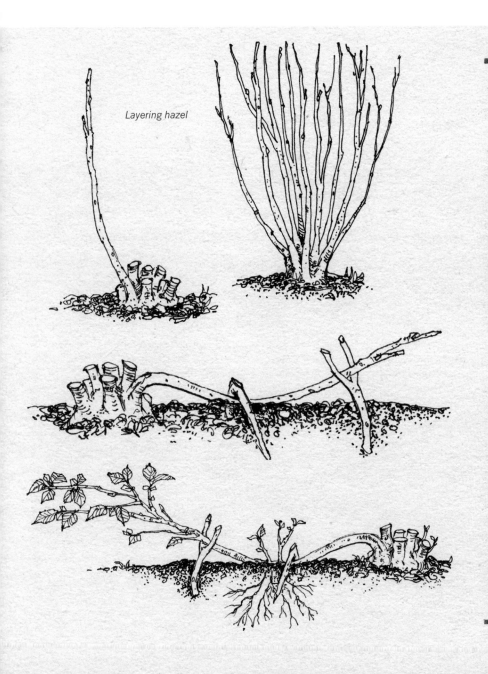

Layering hazel

Cutting derelict or overstood coppice

Cutting derelict coppice can be a challenge but the results are very rewarding. Derelict coppice can be overstood hazel, or a mixed coppice of different species, often with large standards. When I started at Prickly Nut Wood, I cut a number of these copses that had been left uncoppiced for more than 50 years. The woodland was oak standards with a coppice layer of hazel, ash, field maple and hawthorn. The entire coppice layer had made its way to form part of the canopy and some had died by being shaded out by the other species.

Due to the increasing size of the canopy of the standards, the light levels were low to the forest floor and the hazel had grown in a zig-zag pattern, searching for the light through the oak standards. This meant the hazel was often very entwined in the oak canopy branches. A winch becomes an essential item when restoring these copses. First you re-coppice the underwood – this is mainly the hazel and hawthorn layer, and many stems will need winching out of the canopy. Some firewood will come from the thicker stems. Then, having created some space to fell into, you can fell the coppiced field maple and ash. There will be a lot of brash to clear, so a fire or a chipper will be necessary.

Surveying the canopy

Finally you are left with the oak standards, and with the underwood gone it is possible to walk through the woods and survey the canopy and the condition of the standards. First, consider – are there any veteran trees that need to be left to grow old and could be registered on the veteran tree register? Then – are there any standards of poor form (not straight, with large branches coming from low down on the main stem)? These should be marked for felling. Are there any standards with large canopies that are shading too much of the coppice layer below? These should also be marked for felling. Then look at the age structure of the remaining standards. Are they all of a similar age? If possible, try to leave younger standards to come through to replace some of the older standards; leaving a mixed age of standard trees allows for future succession as the wood is managed into the future.

Make sure you have the correct training before felling larger standard trees or contract in a specialist forester who does. They will also be able to organize extracting the timber, which the small woodland owner is usually not equipped to manage. You will need to consider re-fencing the area or engaging a deer stalker and then you can enjoy watching the coppice regeneration unfold, knowing the next time you cut the coppice, in about seven years' time, the work will be so much easier and the cut material more useful.

Woodlander's story: turning derelict coppice into products

Finding product from derelict coppice is often a challenge but one area of oak standards over mixed coppice I cut produced a fruitful array of produce and the woodland has now progressed through two further cuts and a lot of hazel layering to become a productive coppice.

The first cut after the woodland had been left for 50 years produced about 25 cords of firewood. (A cord of timber is 128 cubic ft (3.62 cubic m). The ash was used for chair making and as bracing poles in the roundwood timber frame construction of the local community village shop. The oak standards were milled into planks at the local sawmill.

The waney-edge boards were used as the cladding in the shop and the other planks were air-dried for three months, then kiln dried, machined, tongue-and-grooved and became the floor. The field maple was inoculated with shiitake mushrooms (*Lentinula edodes* – see page 144 for more information on fungi and inoculation) and the hazel was used to weave the wattle frontage on the shop's verandah. The long, straight stems of the hazel went to a cooper (barrel maker) in Liverpool who steamed the hazel and used the rods to tie round the barrels which, in turn, were sold to the Tower of London. All from one derelict coppice!

ABOVE: The Lodsworth Larder. Many parts of the building were made from derelict coppice growing less than a mile away.

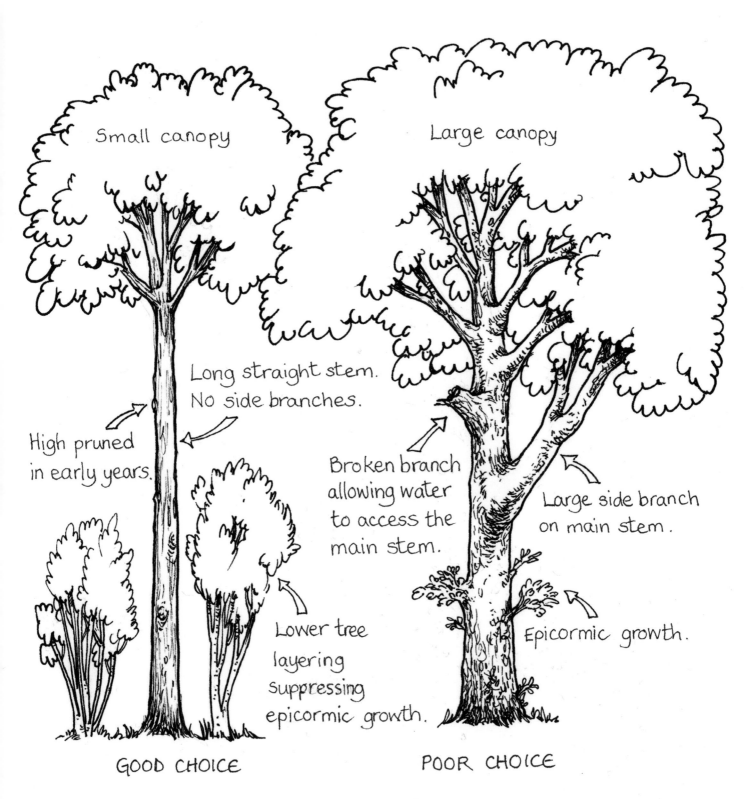

Small canopy

Large canopy

Long straight stem.
No side branches.

High pruned
in early years.

Broken branch
allowing water
to access the
main stem.

Large side branch
on main stem.

Lower tree
layering
suppressing
epicormic growth.

Epicormic growth.

GOOD CHOICE

POOR CHOICE

SELECTING GOOD QUALITY STANDARDS FOR TIMBER.

Cutting longer-cycle coppice

A lot of the sweet chestnut I cut is on a cycle of 30 years or more. This may sound a long cycle for sweet chestnut, but it gives larger diameter poles for roundwood timber framing and shake making as well as good material for cleaving out for post and rail. Other longer cycle copses may be firewood copses of mixed species. Before starting to coppice you need to be clear:

Where are you going to start felling?
If the coppice has an established extraction ride, this will be your main access route in and out of the coppice. I like to fell a row of coppice stools on the opposite side of the ride to the cant I am cutting. Trees on the edge of the ride will have branched out over the ride towards the cant you are going to cut and therefore are likely to cause some of the trees on the edge of the cant you are felling to get hooked up when you start to fell. By removing this row on the opposite side of the ride you will be opening up a larger area to fell into. The next stage will be to thin out smaller stems to leave the main stems more visible. This thinning process aids safe felling, as any branches crossing from one stem to another in the canopy are easier to see after thinning.

When growing coppice on a longer cycle, you are likely to get areas of 'windthrow'. This is where trees have been uprooted or partially uprooted by the wind. This can be severe where large areas are disturbed or more localized with smaller areas occurring throughout the cant you are cutting. Dealing with windthrow is a more dangerous activity than felling upright trees. Stems are likely to be under high levels of tension and compression and it can be quite a puzzle working out the order of which stem to cut first. There are training courses on dealing with windthrown trees and I would recommend taking a course if you have a lot of windthrow in your woodland. The golden rule is not to cut beneath other windthrown stems and start at the stump of the windthrown tree and winch it backwards (in the opposite direction to which it is leaning).

ABOVE: An area of sweet chestnut coppice prior to cutting out the smaller stems.

LEFT: With the smaller stems gone, there is more space to fell the larger stems.

OPPOSITE, CLOCKWISE FROM TOP LEFT: An area of long-cycle coppice after cutting can look a bit devastated at first glance.

A close look and the regrowth is beginning.

By midsummer, the woodland looks vibrant again.

By autumn, the coppice is well recovered.

What are your products?
It is important to know what the bulk of your products are before you start. This will enable you to cross-cut the timber to the required lengths and ease the extraction process. Being organized and clear on your products improves the efficiency of coppicing.

How will you extract the timber?
A lot of the products are carried out to the ride on your shoulder. A 10ft (3m) log for post and rail would be too heavy for most average humans, but cleft into four rails where it has been felled, the individual quartered rails can be more easily carried to the woodland ride. If your copse is for personal firewood, splitting the timber in the cant with wedges reduces the weight you have to carry out and helps speed up the seasoning process. Larger poles, like the timber framing poles I extract, need a winch and a timber crane. Have a clear extraction plan and extract in phases so that you don't build up too much felled timber in the cant.

Where will you store the cut material?
At some point the timber needs to leave the woods. You need to get the timber to a loading bay or place near the roadside where the timber can be loaded onto a vehicle. You need to consider the size of vehicle that will be collecting the timber. Will it be small loads – with a pick-up or road trailer? Will it be a six-wheeler or artic lorry with timber grab? Is there room for the vehicle to turn? If you are going to be cutting and extracting timber from the wood for a number of years, some investment into a hardstanding area near the roadside would be prudent.

If you are cutting for firewood to sell or for personal use, a good plan is to build rustic racks from the coppice poles on the opposite side of the ride from the cant you are cutting. These racks allow airflow under the timber to help the drying process. These can be measured racks, so that the timber is stacked in cords for ease of sale or just a pole between coppice stools on which the firewood poles are elevated off the ground.

What will you do with the brash?
The coppice on the edge of the ride will have far more brash than the poles in the middle of the cant. Provided the stocking rate is good, the poles in the centre of the cant will have very few or no side branches and a small amount of straight top. The brash of larger-rotation coppice is rarely good for faggots as it tends to be sturdy and not easy to pull tight in a faggot jig.

Birch coppice may well produce some useful brash for besom brooms, but beyond that you will need to have a plan for the large volume of brash that comes from the coppice. Traditionally most of the brash was burnt and on some sites a small controlled fire is still acceptable. If you are doing this, try and use a fire site that has been previously used. Chipping the brash will clear it quickly and turn the brash into product if you have a market for the woodchip. I use it to firm up woodland paths that otherwise would turn to mud over the winter.

The other option is to cut the brash into windrows. The brash is laid in a line on the woodland floor (in a similar manner to the drifts mentioned in the 'Cutting On-cycle Hazel Coppice' section). The brash is then cross-cut at close intervals to break it down into smaller pieces that will then break down with the help of woodland fungi into enriching the soil. If using windrows, make sure they are laid out in the same direction as you are extracting timber; you do not want to extract the timber through a series of windrows.

BELOW LEFT: Firewood stacked at the ride side for extraction.

BELOW CENTRE: Chipped brash used on woodland pathways at Prickly Nut Wood.

BELOW RIGHT: A windrow of chopped brash in the copse.

A wide roadside entrance and good loading bay can be a sound investment if there is a lot of timber coming out of the woodland over time.

Woodlander's story: seeing the wood from the trees

The longest products I need from the coppice are timber-framing poles and, depending on the projects I have occurring, they are usually between 12ft (3.65m) and 30ft (9.15m) in length. These poles are cross-cut in length after felling and marked on the end grain with a coloured dot. I keep a key with sizes and colours as sometimes there can be ten or more different products coming out of the coppice and the colour code helps to get the right products to the right place when it comes to extraction. Rails for post and rail are cut to 8ft (2.4m) or 10ft (3m). These can be chosen from timber that has some curve in it, as part of the charm of cleft post and rail is the visual movement in the rails. Posts are cut to a number of sizes, depending on the use and demand, but sizes from 5ft 6in (1.7m) to 8ft 6in (2.6m) are common. Smaller stems are put aside for cleaving into palisade and pales. Clean stems of 4ft (1.2m) are chosen for splitting into laths, and knot-free large-diameter material is cross-cut into 1ft (30cm) lengths for shake making. I cut wood to be seasoned for firewood or charcoal into 6ft (1.8m) lengths. Other products and specific orders come in throughout the cutting season and are marked up accordingly.

Managing for timber

I am a firm believer that a woodland managed with care for timber can also increase biodiversity and the two do not need to be separate management strategies.

If timber is your main focus from the woodland, then ensure timber growing and production is carried out in a manner that avoids any landscape degradation by using appropriate extraction equipment for the size and terrain of the woodland. Try not to extract in poor weather conditions, and be aware of the suggestions in the section on managing for wildlife and increasing biodiversity. This should make it possible to manage a biodiverse timber-producing woodland.

Coppicing is one method of producing small-diameter timber, with larger timber coming from the occasional felling of standards. If you are looking to produce saw logs for sale to sawmills then you will need to be growing some high-forest timber over a longer timescale.

OPPOSITE: High pruning an oak at Prickly Nut Wood.

High-forest silviculture

The management of a forest from planting through to harvesting a tree for timber involves creating the best conditions for the tree to grow. Some trees manage this naturally by the effects of nature on the woodland, but in most cases trees and woodlands need human intervention to produce good-quality timber. These interventions involve pruning and thinning.

Pruning

Pruning is carried out in two stages. Formative pruning involves pruning young trees up to about 10ft (3m) in height. This is to remove forked leader stems and side branches at a young age. Initial close planting will reduce the volume of formative pruning needed but will increase the volume of thinning at a later stage.

High pruning is the second stage of pruning and is carried out using an extendable pole saw that can extend to 20ft (6m). This is to ensure that the main stem of the tree – the part that will become the valuable saw log – is knot-free. Side branches create knots and knots produce weakness in the final timber. High pruning may need to be carried out on a number of occasions, although coppice and shrub species can be encouraged to help to shade the trunk of the high pruned tree. The time taken to high prune a broadleaf tree may increase the value of the saw log by four times when eventually sold.

Woodlander's story: leaving the best for the next generation

My personal role in managing Prickly Nut Wood is that of a steward. I am taking on the management of a woodland that many generations have shaped before me, and my time will be a very short management period in the woodland's life and history. I am often thankful to my predecessors who planted the sweet chestnut coppice and, by hand, dug out the many miles of drainage ditches that work their way through the woods.

I have inherited a selection of standard trees in the woods and, as I mill my own timber, I am very aware of the difference between a good- and poor-quality standard. The majority I have inherited are not good quality as they were not high pruned with that in mind. The young trees I have planted I have high pruned, leaving what should be some good-quality timber to mill in 120 to 150 years' time. One of the real pleasures of working a wood is leaving what you started with in better condition for future generations.

Thinning

Thinning is the process of removing trees to target a final tree or group of trees to reach the ultimate time to harvest the timber. Thinning is based on the natural process of competition in a woodland, where taller trees reaching the canopy will shade out their competitors and the smaller trees die and eventually fall and break down into the soil over time. Thinning is used to target trees most likely to produce the best form and quality of timber by giving the trees the right balance of light. Too much light and they may start to produce epicormic growth and create more side branches; not enough light and they will grow upwards, but not put on any girth.

The choice of when to thin and how often will depend on a number of factors. The species, the initial planting density and soil quality will all affect when to start thinning and how often. Conifers with a shorter cycle to maturity are likely to require more regular thinning compared to broadleaves, which will need thinning less often but over a longer timespan.

Thinning on a large scale can result in beginning with a planting density of 1,000 trees per acre (2,500 trees per hectare) and ending with a final mature crop of 80 trees per acre (200 trees per hectare). There are dangers with large-scale thinning, and the planting of single-species even-aged plantations often become vulnerable to windblow after thinning.

In Great Britain we live on an island with high winds and regular storms; some damage from wind is inevitable in forestry but the industrial plantation model of the last century is a high-risk strategy, as well as a poor environmental choice.

OPPOSITE AND ABOVE: A well-thinned and pruned plantation will provide a good yield of timber at maturity.

Thinning plays an important role in continuous cover forestry. With an irregular forest structure of different age ranges and species, the risk of windthrow is reduced. In continuous cover forestry, where particular trees are being selected for high-quality timber such as oak, the timings and volumes of thinning the shade-tolerant underwood layer of often beech and hornbeam is a skilful practice.

If your management focus in your small woodland is to produce high-value timber or if you have purchased a woodland with an existing plantation and are uncertain how to proceed, then some professional advice on thinning may be prudent.

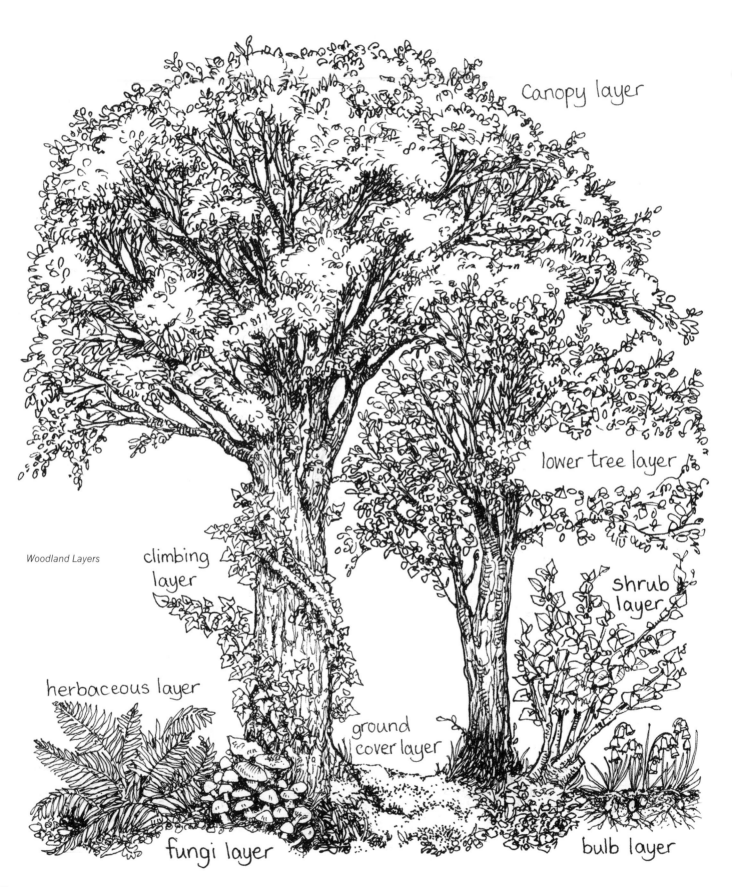

Canopy layer

lower tree layer

Woodland Layers

climbing layer

shrub layer

herbaceous layer

ground cover layer

fungi layer

bulb layer

Managing for wildlife and biodiversity

Management strategies for increasing biodiversity can work alongside more commercial woodland activities. By factoring in ride management and leaving more deadwood and clearings, introducing coppicing and adapting the layer structure and diversity of tree species, a significant improvement and increase in biodiversity can be seen relatively quickly.

Species and age structure

If a woodland is lacking in tree species diversity, then adjusting the balance by removing some of the existing trees and replanting with different ones will help increase biodiversity. Native trees that have coexisted with our native flora and fauna will be more supportive of invertebrates and will be important food plants for moths or butterflies. Always consider incorporating some native species into the woodland. A mixed native hedgerow planted around the edge will create a nesting habitat for many birds.

Varying the age structure in the woodland will also help to increase biodiversity. Age structure helps create layers within the woodland. The drawing opposite shows an ideal layer structure of a woodland. There are eight layers, and the more of these layers that are established, the more likely there will be an increase in biodiversity.

The canopy layer is the high forest layer, and includes oak or beech. Below that is the lower tree layer, where species such as hawthorn or mountain ash (rowan) will be outgrown by the high forest canopy layer. The shrub layer, with its guelder rose or dogwood, among others, sits just below this. Further below lies the herbaceous layer, including dog's mercury or foxglove. After that, we have the ground-cover layer, where you will find wood anemone or primrose. Even further below this is the bulb layer, with bluebells and wild garlic. Throughout the soil and in deadwood is the fungi layer. Meanwhile, working its way up through the trees, the climbing layer consists of the likes of honeysuckle or ivy. Don't forget the mosses and lichens that are both ground cover and climbing species!

Take a walk through your woodland and see how many layers are visible. If the woodland is predominantly one or two layers, then altering species and age structure will help increase the woodland layers and associated biodiversity.

ABOVE LEFT: The intricately made nest of the long-tailed tit, often hidden.

ABOVE RIGHT: Common lizards are abundant at Prickly Nut Wood.

Coppice cycles for wildlife

Coppice cycles have traditionally involved cutting on a particular cycle for the size of poles needed for a particular craft. At Prickly Nut Wood most of my sweet chestnut coppice is cut on a long cycle of around 30 years. This provides large poles for roundwood timber framing, roofing shakes, post-and-rail fencing and a range of other craft produce. In working long cycles, the woodland benefits from a lot of shade around the chestnut stools, which harbour a healthy population of mosses, ferns and lichens. These are the bryophyte community for which the woodland is a Site of Special Scientific Interest (SSSI). Shorter cycles can provide more habitat for wildflowers and butterflies. Hazel coppice is traditionally cut on a seven-year cycle for hurdle making but in the south of England with warmer summers, the hazel is growing more quickly and is often of the right diameter to cut every five years. A five-year cycle will help create a good build-up of wildflowers and butterfly habitat but will not be ideal if dormice are also present, which like hazel on a longer cycle of 10 to 15 years. Balancing the different needs of different species can be challenging, particularly in a small

TOP LEFT: Moss. TOP RIGHT: Flag iris (Iris pseudacorus) is an important waterplant for emerging dragonflies to dry their wings before their maiden flight. ABOVE LEFT: Paradise for amphibians. ABOVE CENTRE: Bugle (Ajuga reptans). ABOVE RIGHT: Turkey tail fungi (Trametes versicolor).

wood where there may not be the area to have different rotations for different targeted conservation species. This is where a management plan for a large area of woodland is beneficial, even if the land is owned by a number of different landowners, each with a small plot of land.

Pearl-bordered fritillary butterfly.

Woodlander's story: butterflies

Butterflies have shaped my management at Prickly Nut Wood. For 50 years prior to my arrival, coppicing stopped and the rides became overgrown with trees, which reduced the light to the woodland floor and in turn reduced the food plants for butterflies. In making my management decisions for the woodland, it has always been a balance between conservation and timber production.

With coppicing it is a symbiotic relationship and as I have opened up the rides and started to widen some of them, and with the increased light levels due to coppicing, the butterfly population in the wood has increased. Looking at butterfly life cycles, the habitat they need and the type of plants they need at different stages in their life cycle enables me to make management decisions that benefit butterflies as part of my woodland management plan. These decisions are often simple changes that have large benefits.

For example, I encourage honeysuckle, especially among trees and coppice regrowth on the edge of rides. Many foresters cut honeysuckle back because, as it twists around a stem, it affects the shape of the tree. I use the twisted stems for rustic furniture but what I have noticed most is the increase in the white admiral butterfly, whose sole food plant is honeysuckle.

Understanding the needs of a particular butterfly and helping to create that habitat can form a regular part of a woodland management plan. Another area of the woodland is currently being considered by butterfly conservationists as a reintroduction site for the small pearl-bordered fritillary butterfly (*Boloria selene*) due to the increase in numbers of the dog violet (*Viola riviniana*) and the woodland's general suitable habitat for the butterfly species. Creating beneficial habitats should go hand in hand with woodland management activities.

THIS PAGE: The woodland awakes
to the unfurling of ferns.

OPPOSITE: Yellow archangel
(Lamium galeobdolon).

Deadwood

I am a keen gardener, but a woodland is not a garden, so don't over-tidy the woodland floor!

An abundance of deadwood for beetles and other invertebrates will ensure good habitat and a healthy food chain throughout the woodland. There are many types of deadwood habitat that can be created as part of routine forest management operations. Standing deadwood should be left, where possible. A large, standing deadwood tree will be an evolving habitat for many species. I leave standing deadwood stems in the coppice and these also work as important habitat for woodpeckers and calling posts for nightjars.

I girdle (ring-bark) trees in the woodland. This process of removing the bark and bast all the way around the tree cuts off the flow of sap from the roots to the branches, resulting in the tree slowly dying above where the bark and bast is removed. The tree usually breaks into leaf and then dies off over a period of a couple of months, creating a unique habitat during that period and beyond. I usually girdle trees that would be otherwise too awkward to fell, for example, a large coppiced stem that has grown up into the canopy of a standard tree and would need a winch to remove it. This creates habitat and eases the management of the woodland in one process.

Deadwood piles on the ground create another important habitat. I always leave piles of deadwood throughout the woodland. As they decay over the years, they create unique habitats for many species. I also use windrows in the woods. These well-chopped piles of brash and small wood soon break down and create linear mounds of decaying organic matter – they are frequented by invertebrates and encouraged in their return to the soil by woodland fungi. All of these different deadwood habitats throughout the woodland greatly improve biodiversity and add to the rich build-up of organic matter of the woodland soils.

OPPOSITE: This old beech tree creates a wonderful deadwood habitat for many different species

BELOW: Standing deadwood left after coppicing at Prickly Nut Wood.

ABOVE: A three-tiered ride.

OPPOSITE: Biodiversity is enhanced where woodlands meet the edge of a stream or river.

Woodland rides and clearings

Clearings create areas where light reaches the woodland soil and in turn stimulates new growth of wildflowers and trees. If a clearing is maintained by cutting it annually or twice a year, the wildflowers will build up in numbers and diversity and the young trees will eventually give up for being constantly cut back hard.

A good-sized clearing, especially if linked to a wide ride, will provide good diversity and butterfly habitat. Rides, where possible, should be cut with wide tiered edges. A three-zone system is good for light, with the first zone each side of the ride being cut on an annual basis – this will support wildflowers and grasses; the second zone is usually cut every three years and will contain a mixture of ferns, herbaceous perennials and grasses; and the third zone will be cut as coppice on about a five- to seven-year cycle with high forest beyond.

This tiered management maximizes the range of habitats along the ride edge. As well as the tiered three-zone system, 'scallops' cut along the ride edge will extend the tiered areas into the woodland, creating more edge between habitats. Scallops are a bit like a lay-by cut near the edge of a ride; they create small rideside clearings, which can then be cut when cutting the zones on the rideside.

Water

Water within a woodland will provide a unique habitat and, if created, will very quickly become rich in biodiversity. If you are considering creating a pond or pond system through your woodland, consider the soil type and whether the soil will naturally hold water or will need to be lined. A heavy clay soil will naturally hold water if puddled. This process involves working the soil into a sticky, thick porridge consistency with your feet prior to adding water. The process removes air from the soil and creates a good binding clay layer. This can be successfully done by fencing a pig in the pond area – it will carry out the work for you!

If your woodland has a natural slope and a stream, a few small ponds can be created to hold water as it flows through the woods. Ponds will need looking after, but to increase biodiversity it is good to have ponds at different phases of maintenance. A freshly dug pond will often have clearer water with less build-up of leaf mould in the base of the pond than a pond that hasn't been dug out for 20 years, but both provide unique habitats for different species. I was astonished how quickly a pond I dug out was found by so many species. In the first year the pond was colonized by frogs, toads, two species of newt (common and palmate), a large number of water beetles and skaters, dragonflies and damselflies and was visited by swallows and bats.

Ponds attract a variety of wildlife and increase the species diversity of a woodland.

TOOLS FOR WOODLAND MANAGEMENT

There is a wide range of tools that can be used for woodland management. A short-rotation coppice woodland can be managed purely with hand tools whereas mature high forest is likely to need some assistance from larger machinery. For small woodlands it is often a case of purchasing what you need and then hiring in machinery or contractors for specific tasks where the volume of work cannot justify an outright purchase.

Cutting and felling tools

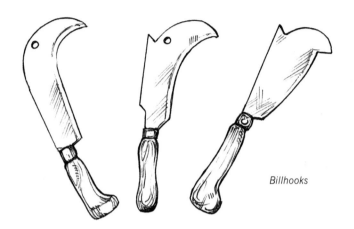

Billhooks

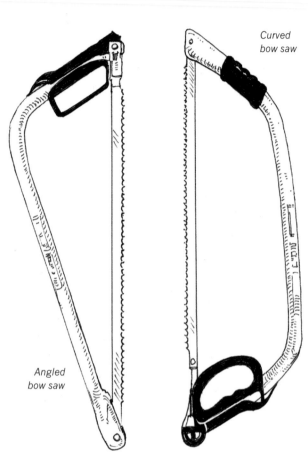

Curved bow saw

Angled bow saw

Billhook

From the time we could forge steel, the billhook has been the 'go-to' tool of the countryside. An experienced woodlander can manage a hazel coppice and convert the cut stems to hurdles using just a billhook. This inexpensive tool should be in every woodlander's toolkit. There are regional patterns and a variety of makers. Try and find a properly forged tool as it will hold a better edge – there is a good secondhand market for billhooks.

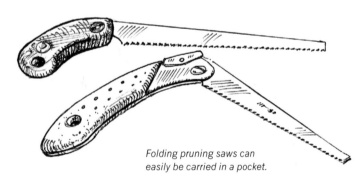

Folding pruning saws can easily be carried in a pocket.

Pruning saw

Pruning saws come either folded or sheathed and cut on the pull stroke. They are lightweight and easy to carry in and out of the woods, either in a deep pocket or attached to a belt. Long-handled versions with extendable poles can reach over 20ft (6m).

Even-tooth blade and raker saw blade

Bow saws

Modern bow saws come in a range of sizes and both the more traditionally curved bow and angled bow saw are useful for a multitude of woodland tasks. The angled saw is better for coppicing as it can fit between the coppice stems.

There are two blades that are commonly sold with most bow saws: a blade with even teeth and a 'raker' saw blade. The raker saw blade is better for cutting green wood as it is designed to deal with the moisture and soft bark that freshly cut branches have.

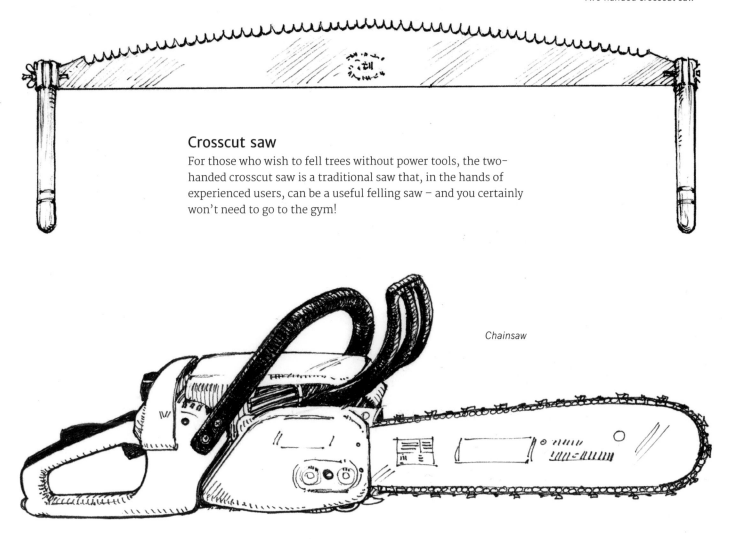

Crosscut saw

For those who wish to fell trees without power tools, the two-handed crosscut saw is a traditional saw that, in the hands of experienced users, can be a useful felling saw – and you certainly won't need to go to the gym!

Chainsaw

Chainsaw

The chainsaw is a fast and efficient saw and an essential tool in managing a woodland. Chainsaws come in a range of bar sizes appropriate to the task. Chainsaws are also potentially dangerous for the inexperienced and should always be used with the appropriate personal protective equipment (PPE), which includes chainsaw boots, helmet with visor, chainsaw protective trousers and chainsaw gloves.

Before using a chainsaw, I advise participating in a chainsaw training course – this will give you the necessary instruction for using the saw safely and also teach you important felling cuts to enable safe felling of trees. In Great Britain these

courses can lead to an assessment carried out by a City and Guilds (NPTC) assessor and, once passed, you will be given a 'skills card' that allows you to use a chainsaw in other people's woodlands. Once qualified it is a ticket towards potential employment.

Although most chainsaws that are used in woodlands are petrol two-stroke saws, there is a growing range of battery saws that are improving in quality and performance. These can be used for felling small trees or firewood processing. With the improvement of these saws, I hope that over the next few years they will reach a standard of power whereby they can replace the need for petrol saws in small-scale woodland management.

Axes

Axes come in many shapes and sizes but the main one I find useful in managing a woodland is a felling axe. This has a flared blade and a long handle of about 36in (91.5cm) and was the traditional tool for felling chestnut coppice prior to the arrival of the chainsaw.

A snedding axe, often a 'Kent pattern', was the traditional axe for removing branches from felled trees and coppice poles. The handles are usually 24–30in (60–76cm) in length. A splitting axe is the best tool for splitting logs – this has wedge-shaped areas in the middle of the blade, which widens the angle as the blade enters the log and helps to facilitate the split. The axe I use the most for shaping wood is the side axe. Side axes have only one side bevelled; the other is entirely flat. This allows the axe to cut into the grain with each stroke whereas a double-bevelled axe will pull away. They come in left- and right-handed versions and have a short handle of around 12in (30cm). The side axe is held at the neck, just below the blade, and the weight of the head does the work, using your hand as a pivot. The side axe can be used for pointing and shaping all wood, from poles down to more detailed work.

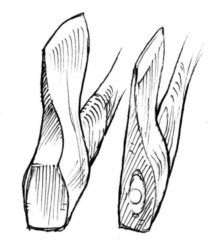

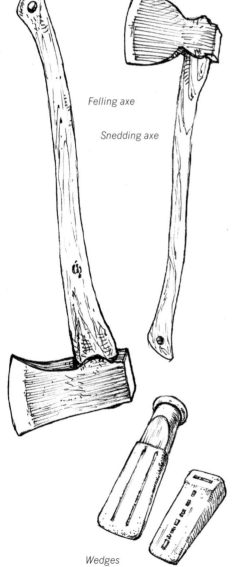

Felling axe

Snedding axe

Heads of splitting axe (left) and side axe (right).

Wedges

A felling lever with cant hook for rotating trees.

Wedges

Wedges come in different sizes and are used to aid with the felling of trees. I use small 6in (15cm) wedges for assisting with felling backward-leaning, large-diameter chestnut coppice and the larger wedges for directional felling of larger trees. The larger wedges are used with a long-handled sledgehammer. **Please get instruction on a chainsaw course before attempting any felling.**

Wedges are also used in cleaving wood – the process of splitting longer lengths of wood by forcing the fibres apart with a number of wedges. Some wedges are designed as twist wedges for this purpose, as they are hammered into the log they twist, opening up the cleave.

Felling lever

These are used to aid the felling of trees once the correct felling cuts have been made. The lever is inserted into the back of the cut and an upward motion on the handle helps push the tree over while the process is still being controlled by the hinge that was established while making the felling cuts. The hook on the felling lever is used to help free 'hooked-up' trees by rotating the base of the felled tree with part of the hinge still attached. (A chainsaw felling course will teach you to make these cuts and use this tool safely and accurately.)

The wedge-shaped head of a splitting axe makes this the best type of axe for splitting logs.

Timber moving and extraction tools

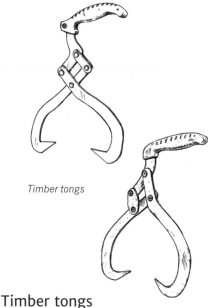

Timber tongs

Timber tongs

Timber tongs are designed to help aid the picking up and dragging of logs. The operator standing next to the log bends their knees and pushes the tongs down onto the log. The jaws open and when the operator lifts or drags, the tongs have grabbed the log. Very useful in small-scale extraction or clearing up a felling site.

Two-person timber tongs

These are designed along the same principles as the timber tongs, but have larger jaws and a long horizontal wooden handle. They are used for lifting and dragging larger pieces of timber. Two people stand, one each side of the timber, holding each end of the wooden handle. They press the jaws down against the top of the log, which open, and grab the log; they then lift and walk, dragging the log with them.

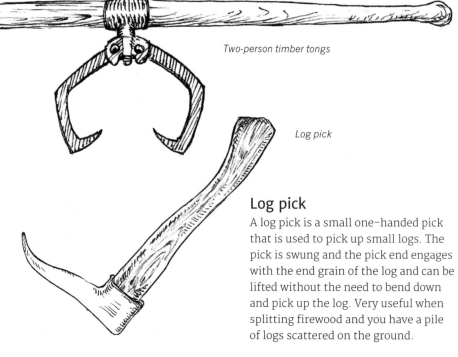

Two-person timber tongs

Log pick

Log pick

A log pick is a small one-handed pick that is used to pick up small logs. The pick is swung and the pick end engages with the end grain of the log and can be lifted without the need to bend down and pick up the log. Very useful when splitting firewood and you have a pile of logs scattered on the ground.

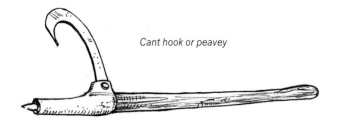

Cant hook or peavey

Double cant hook

The double cant hook works with the same principle as a single cant hook but has a second hook attached near the first and a sliding ratchet to engage the second hook while disengaging the first. This allows a single operator to roll a log uphill without the risk of the log rolling back on the operator when the hook is released. I use this tool when working on my own and loading timber up a ramp onto the sawmill.

Double cant hook

Cant hook or peavey

The cant hook or peavey is made up of a strong wooden handle (ash or hickory) and an attached hook. The handle is shaped with a point on the end nearest the hook, and it is used for both separating logs from a pile and for rolling large logs. When two people are working together on a large piece of timber with one at each end, they can work together and roll a significant weight of timber uphill with minimum effort. The cant hook works on the principle of 'levers', and is a well-designed and engineered tool. A cant hook is a favourite tool of mine and one I use often for moving timber. One person with a cant hook can move timber that would take three people without one.

Hand winch

Log arch

This is designed to lift a length of timber off the ground and then move the timber on the attached wheels. A manual log arch involves pushing the arch over the length of timber and lifting the handles up in the air. This brings the jaws down in contact with the log that open around it. When you then bring the handles back down, the log is lifted and is held in the jaws at one end and by the support under the handles. A little practice is needed to choose the right position on the log to engage the jaws, but you soon get used to it. This arch is best used on solid ground or hard woodland rides as once the log is lifted you need to manually push or pull the arch. Larger arches can be pulled by horses, or adapted with a towing hitch for a quad bike or small tractor.

Hand winch

These come in different sizes, from the small 'Lugall' style winches that are lightweight through to the heavy duty 'Tirfor' style that can move many tonnes of timber. Both types are based around a steel cable and are secured to a support (often a tree or stump) with a strop. The lightweight winches are useful for helping drag back hooked-up trees while felling and are easy to carry in and out of the woods. The larger 'Tirfor' type will extract large trees but are heavy to move around due to the weight of the thicker steel cable. Hand winches are low maintenance but slow when used for extraction.

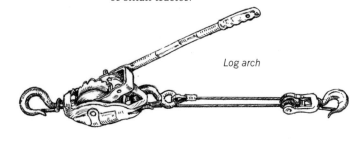

Log arch

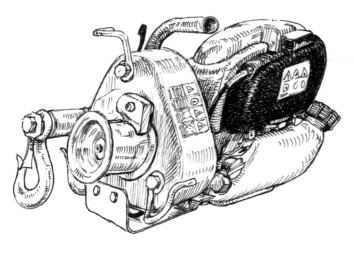

Portable capstan winch

Portable capstan winch

This winch is becoming increasingly popular in small-scale forestry. The winch consists of a small and very fuel-economical four-stroke petrol engine, which drives the capstan. Around the capstan is looped a lightweight winch rope. Once the operator puts tension on the rope, the capstan engages and draws the rope towards the winch, pulling the attached log. If the operator releases the rope, the winch stops pulling as there is no tension on the capstan.

I use this winch a lot for lighter weight timber extraction. This is because the rope – not being a steel cable – is lightweight and means carrying the winch into the woods is not a struggle. But the main advantage of this winch is that – being a capstan winch – the rope does not need to coil up like a drum winch, which means you can winch your timber the full distance of the length of your rope. I have approximately 500ft (150m) of rope and can pull out logs from some of the more difficult areas to access in my woods.

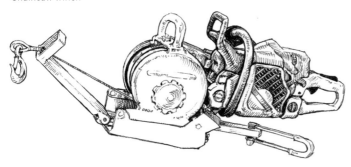

Chainsaw winch

Chainsaw winch

This is a useful winch as it is lightweight and there is no need for the maintenance of an extra engine. It works by removing the cutting bar and chain from your saw and attaching the chainsaw drive to the winch. Make sure your chainsaw is of suitable power and compatibility for the winch. The top brands are well engineered and this can be useful for regular use and as an emergency winch.

PTO tractor winch

These winches are driven by the tractor PTO (power take-off) and are attached to the tractor three-point linkage. There is a blade that pushes down into the ground to help anchor the tractor. This is a drum winch and has a heavy duty steel cable. Many models are available, both with manual and remote control operation. Most have the option to attach the winched log to the blade frame with logging chains so that when the three-point linkage is lifted, the lumber is elevated and can be skidded out behind the tractor.

PTO tractor winch

Winching accessories

All of these accessories will help with the winching and extraction of timber. It is important to check that they are genuine forestry accessories and have been load tested for the work you are undertaking.

Nose cone

I use a nose cone when winching. The logging chain slides through the end of the nose cone and attaches to the log. When the winch is operated, the log is pulled into the open end and it is the pointed end of the cone that moves first, bouncing off any obstacles and ensuring the log travels with ease towards the winch. The nose cone will reduce damage caused by the log digging into the ground when being winched as well as reduce the frequency of the log getting stuck against stumps or standing trees.

Nose cone

Logging chains

These are chains that wrap around a log. They have a hook at one end, which the chain is inserted into, and the chain pulls tight around the log like a noose. The other end of the chain can have different attachments depending on the type of winch you are using. It may have an eye for attaching to a winch hook or a slider that fits over a winch cable when multiple logs are being extracted. Make sure to use the appropriate load-tested logging chain for the size of timber you are extracting.

Logging chains

Strops and shackles

Strops are load rated and flexible and come with loops at each end. These can be wrapped around a tree or stump to then anchor a winch. They are colour coded for their load ratings. Shackles are used for joining strops and are also load rated. They have a removable threaded bolt for locking/unlocking the shackle.

Strops and shackles

Snatch blocks

These pulleys can be strapped to a tree or other anchor point. The pulley needs to correspond to the size of rope or cable being used. They are load rated and used often where the winching is not in a straight line.

Snatch blocks

Log chutes

Log chutes

These have been used in many forms to move logs. Gravity and water are great movers of weight, so a traditional log chute uses both. Modern log chutes are made from interlocking plastic sections, either round or half round, and are laid out so the chute works its way down a hillside. Water is a helpful addition but the plastic chutes are slippery enough to run dry. Be aware that logs can exit the chute at fast speeds.

Log grapple

Log grapple

This hydraulic set of jaws runs off a tractor's three-point linkage and hydraulic system. The tractor reverses up to the log and grabs one end with the grapple – the linkage then lifts that end of the log up, allowing the tractor to skid the log out of the woodland.

Draught bit and traces

Timber extraction with horses

The most sustainable form of timber extraction without doubt comes from using horses. The traditional use of 'draught bit and traces' allows delicate extraction, skidding individual logs between trees where only a clearance of 3ft (1m) is needed, to where they can be picked up later with a forwarder. The advantages of using horses for timber extraction are many but in particular the lack of damage to the woodland floor that large-scale forestry equipment often causes means that for many sensitive and nature conservation sites, 'snigging', or horse extraction, is the chosen method.

Development of equipment, especially from Scandinavia, where the value of horses in forestry has never been forgotten, has produced log arches and forwarders that are well designed for the horse's well-being and increase efficiency in the volume of timber that can be extracted.

Different breeds can be used for different extraction: a cob can successfully help with lighter weight extraction of coppice poles whereas for larger timber and tenacity of work, a heavy horse will be needed. The stocky and powerful Ardennes seems to have the perfect balance in weight and size for a forestry horse. Modern timber trailers with a separate engine and hydraulics can be pulled by horses, allowing efficient

Horse logging arch

loading of timber with a forestry crane but leaving minimal soil disturbance in its wake.

Alpine tractor and ATV/quad forwarder

There has been an increase in choice of small-scale extraction equipment for forestry. In particular, forestry trailers and cranes are being designed for using with small ATVs (all-terain vehicles).

These can be a good solution if you are managing a small woodland and extracting a small amount of timber for firewood each year. Be sure to get a suitable size and weight ratio between the ATV and the trailer. It is easy to choose a larger trailer when it is empty but imagine it full of logs and you are pulling it uphill!

The alpine tractor, which gets its name for its stability in mountainous regions, is a more powerful option but, provided you choose a reversible model, it can be a very efficient low-impact forwarder. Damage caused in woodlands by machinery is often caused by too large a machine to be appropriate for the woodland, the lack of use of brash mats in coniferous woods (brash mats are where foliage is laid down on the woodland floor while machinery is extracting timber and then removed afterwards) or by the turning around of machinery in the woodland.

Reversable alpine tractors remove the need to turn the tractor in the woodland; instead they have a turntable where the steering column and seat can be turned 180 degrees and have a separate brake and clutch available in this reversed position. So it is easy to drive into the woodland with your empty trailer in front of you, load up with timber, then turn the seat and steering column and drive out the way you came in. The introduction of a turntable and the ability not to have to turn around in the woodland makes the alpine tractor a good option.

Quad bike with small timber trailer and crane.

Horse-drawn forwarder with timber crane.

Woodlander's story: extracting oak by horse

The times I have had the pleasure of extracting timber with horses rank at the top of my woodland experiences. One spring, I had been asked to rebuild a barn in a local woodland. We had felled 60 oak trees as part of a thinning of standards over a large area of coppice and had to extract them from where they were felled, between about 300–600ft (100–200m) to where we had brought in a mobile sawmill to convert them to beams and cladding for a timber-framed barn.

The horses, two Ardennes called Monty and Dylan, came from The Working Horse Trust. Using mainly a low-wheeled forwarder and a single horse to pull steadily over the period of a couple of days (although we did double up on the biggest trees), the felled oaks that

had laid scattered across the woodland floor found themselves in a large, orderly stack alongside the sawmill.

The horses were well trained and guided by a calm and experienced hand and the process felt like a natural extension of the woodland cycle. Woodlanders and timber framers, we all joined in the experience and took turns under a watchful eye to lead the horses pulling the forwarder back through the ancient woodland to the barn site on the edge. Once all the logs were extracted and the horses had returned home, I walked through the woodland at the end of a spring day, gratified by the experience I had been part of and deeply satisfied to see nothing but hoofprints left marking the woodland rides.

Peeling tools

With your timber felled and extracted, if you are not selling it on as lumber then your next process will be to peel it.

Debarking spade

There are a few different designs of debarking spade or spud available. They come with or without a handle. I prefer to buy them without a handle, as the handles tend to be shorter than I care to use. Before debarking a log, look at the direction it has grown by observing any taper or the direction of growth of knots. Start debarking from the bottom of the log to the top – this way, if you go over a knot, it will take it off cleanly rather than rip out if you go from top to bottom.

A debarking spade has a semi-sharp edge: sharp enough to remove the bark but not too sharp so that it digs into the wood.

Peeling logs using a debarking spade.

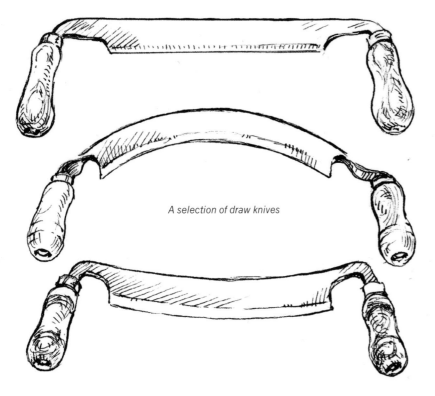

A selection of draw knives

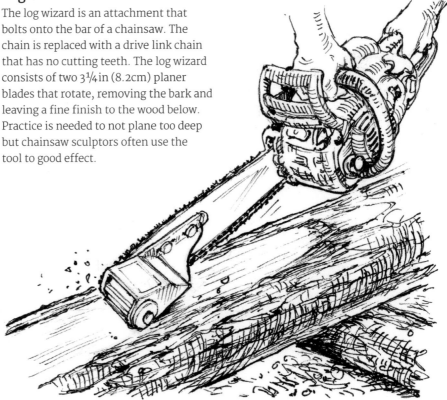

Bark peeling iron

Peeling iron

A handheld peeling iron has a slightly curved lip and is used to lift bark from freshly felled logs in the spring. This is the time of year when the bark lifts more easily from the log due to the fresh flow of sap beneath it. The peeling iron can be used to remove whole rounds of bark as you can work it around the log once its tip is well under the bark and bast. This is a useful tool when bark is wanted as a product rather than just removing it for the benefit of using the peeled timber.

Draw knife

A draw knife gives a beautiful hand-peeled finish to wood and is my favourite peeling tool. When I am peeling round poles for timber framing, I take off the bark and bast with the debarking spade and then finish the poles with a draw knife. This way I am not blunting the tool on the rough bark but saving it for the quality of finish. Almost all craft projects where you are starting with a felled tree will use a draw knife at some point in the process. A draw knife can be flat bladed or curved, and some have straight or cranked handles; it is a personal choice which draw knife feels right to the individual.

Log wizard

The log wizard is an attachment that bolts onto the bar of a chainsaw. The chain is replaced with a drive link chain that has no cutting teeth. The log wizard consists of two 3¼ in (8.2cm) planer blades that rotate, removing the bark and leaving a fine finish to the wood below. Practice is needed to not plane too deep but chainsaw sculptors often use the tool to good effect.

Mechanical peeler

There are a few companies making mechanical peelers and the designs and safety have moved on from the older designs that I used in the woods 30 years ago. Some have their own engines whereas many attach to the PTO and three-point linkage of a tractor. They consist of a large circular disc with planer blades, not dissimilar to a woodchipper, except the pole is rotated sideways past the spinning blade to remove the bark whereas with a woodchipper the wood is drawn in with the end grain meeting the blades.

Some of the peelers are semi-automatic, meaning once the log is fed into the peeler, it will draw the log through, turning it as it goes; others are manual and mean spinning the log by hand as it contacts the blade. The finish is clearly a machine finish and cannot match the quality of finish that hand tools bring but if you are peeling large numbers of fencing posts where the finished look is not so important, it could be a good investment. Some models also point posts as well as peel.

Woodlander's story: spring bast removal

Each year as spring arrives and the sap flows strongly up through the trees, I fell a few last chestnut poles to harvest bark for seat weaving. It peels off easily at this time of the year but it is the bast (the under bark) I use.

First, I lightly remove the outer bark using a spokeshave, being careful not to cut too deep and affect the bast below. Once the outer bark is removed, I use a sharp knife and a 1in (25mm) thick ruler and cut through the bast to the wood below. This leaves a series of long lines down the length of the pole. Using a peeling iron, I work the tool under the bast and lift the lengths of bast from the pole. These can be woven fresh to form the seats of stools and chairs, or coiled up and dried out and stored, ready to be re-soaked and used later.

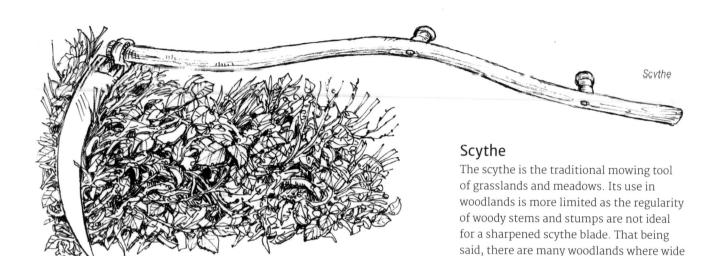

Scythe

Scythe

The scythe is the traditional mowing tool of grasslands and meadows. Its use in woodlands is more limited as the regularity of woody stems and stumps are not ideal for a sharpened scythe blade. That being said, there are many woodlands where wide grass and wildflower strips are encouraged for butterfly conservation and a scythe can be the perfect tool for peaceful mowing of these rides. There is a strong renaissance in scything and in particular the importing and use of Austrian hand-forged scythe blades.

Ride management tools

For small woodland owners who are looking at improving biodiversity and wildlife management as a main objective, good ride management is likely to be a key activity.

Brushcutter

A brushcutter is usually fitted with a three-sided blade. This is particularly good for cutting through areas of bramble and thin woody stems and can be useful in cutting back along ditches and ride edges. The brushcutter can also be used as a clearing saw, when fitted with a circular saw blade for cutting back thicker woody stems. As with most machinery, buy good quality if you can. My brushcutter has just passed 30 years of age!

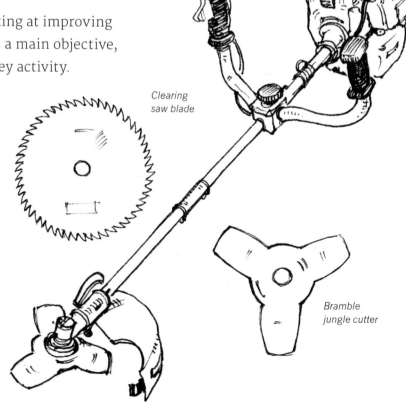

Brushcutter

Clearing saw blade

Bramble jungle cutter

Brushmower

The brushmower is a powerful machine designed for cutting rough areas with stems up to 2in (50mm) thick in diameter. They usually have two large wheels at the back and an angled front for pushing over saplings prior to cutting them. They are well designed to cope with hitting stumps and stones, so those hidden obstacles often concealed beneath regrowth shouldn't cause a problem.

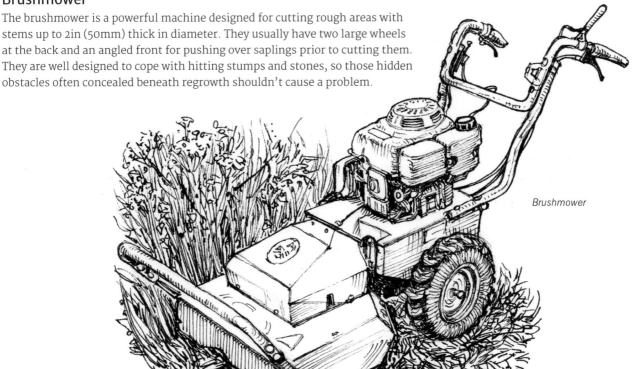

Brushmower

Two-wheel tractor and implements

A two-wheel tractor could be a suitable choice for ride management as well as offering an array of attachments that could be useful in all forms of woodland management. The two-wheel tractor is a walk-behind machine with a number of different attachments mainly designed for agricultural land or smallholdings. In a woodland, useful attachments include a scythe cutting bar, a mulching mower, a small trailer, woodchipper and a stump grinder. If you have pasture or agricultural land as well as woodland, the two-wheel tractor could be a good option.

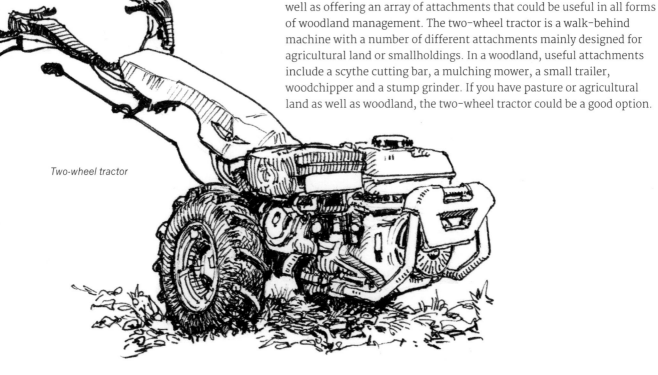

Two-wheel tractor

Timber measuring and marking tools

Although some can be quite specialist, here I recommend a few useful tools to improve accuracy in measuring and marking timber.

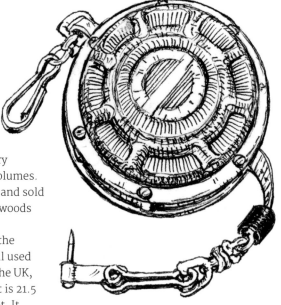

Timber tape

Timber tapes

Logging tapes are steel retractable tape measures that clip onto your belt or the belt loop of your trousers. They have a spike on one end with a 90-degree joint so that the spike can be inserted into the end grain of the log. As you walk down the log, the tape unwinds and you can measure and mark accurately prior to cross-cutting. They come in imperial, metric or both.

Girthing tapes are unique tapes used for measuring the diameter of a log. The measurement is either in metric or imperial reduced by the value of π. The tape is used by measuring the circumference of the tree stem and it will convert that value into the diameter to the nearest unit. These can be very useful when calculating timber volumes.

Conifers are usually measured and sold by the cubic metre, whereas hardwoods are often still sold by the hoppus foot. Edward Hoppus introduced the measurement in 1736 and it is still used widely in the timber industry in the UK, USA and Canada. The hoppus foot is 21.5 per cent less than a true cubic foot. It is a measurement favoured by sawmills as the 21.5 per cent allows for the slab wood waste, which is the four cuts on the sawmill that turn a cylindrical log into a squared beam. Hence the buyer is only paying for the usable timber. The formula for the volume of timber is: pi x radius squared x height ($V=\pi r2h$).

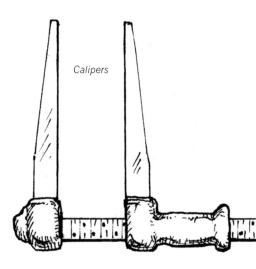

Calipers

Calipers

Forestry calipers are large calipers used for measuring the diameter of trees, both standing and felled. Using these for measuring the diameter of standing timber, along with a clinometer for measuring height, it is possible to estimate volumes of timber within a woodland.

Timber scribe or race knife

This is a most useful little tool for marking timber. It has a small 'U' shaped cutting edge, a bit like a small gouge and the blade folds into the wooden handle, so it is easy to carry in your pocket. I use it mainly for marking where to

cut tree lengths when I am cross-cutting felled timber for products. It works by scratching a clear mark in the timber, removing the bark. The mark it leaves is a similar width to the width of a chainsaw bar. With a logging tape and the timber scribe, I can accurately mark up timber prior to cutting.

Using a timber tape and race knife to mark a log for accurate cross-cutting.

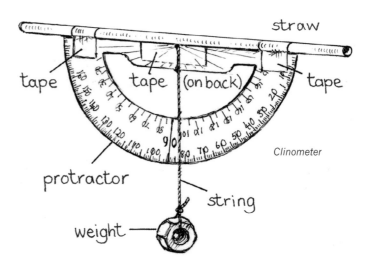

Clinometer

Clinometer

A clinometer is an instrument used for measuring angles and, along with a measuring tape, can accurately measure the height of a standing tree. There is a range of clinometers on the market, from manual through to digital, and even some smartphone apps that can be used for tree height measurement. For many woodland owners, a simple clinometer made from a protractor, a small stick, a piece of string and a washer will suffice.

By holding the clinometer and looking from your eyeline along the stick to the top of the tree (or the point on the tree you want to measure to), the string with weight will give you the angle on the protractor. Having measured the distance you are from the tree and the height of your eyeline from the ground, you can use the formula shown below.

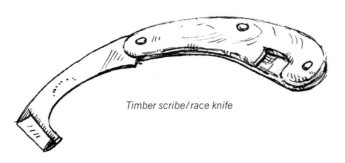

Timber scribe/race knife

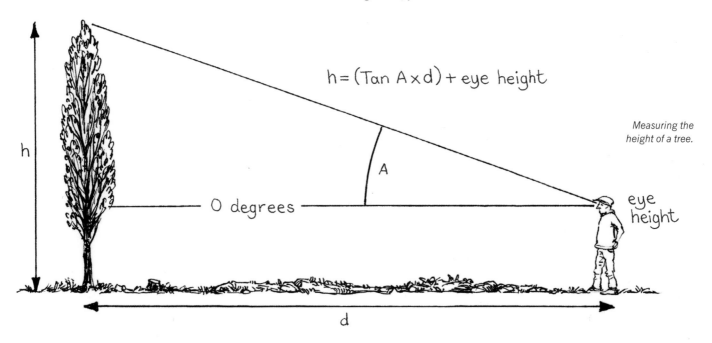

$$h = (\text{Tan } A \times d) + \text{eye height}$$

Measuring the height of a tree.

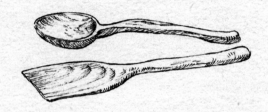

SELLING TIMBER

Managing a small woodland will undoubtedly bring you some timber. This may be small amounts that you convert to logs for your own use or it may be larger amounts of timber that you need to sell on to a buyer. This could be a once-in-a-decade activity as you thin and remove trees, or a regular annual felling programme, depending on your management plan for your woodland.

Types of timber to sell

You will need to decide whether you are going to carry out the work yourself or hire a contractor and at what point you want to sell the timber. If, for example, you have a 'plantation on an ancient woodland site' and need to fell and remove the introduced tree species, you could sell the timber 'standing', 'felled', 'extracted to woodside', 'extracted to roadside' or you could consider adding value to it by conversion to timber products. One key thing to remember is that in the UK, if you sell the timber without adding value to it, it is exempt from income tax and corporation tax. Once you add value to it, it becomes taxable.

Selling standing timber

If you do not have the skills and tools to fell your own timber, then getting in a contractor to buy the standing timber will be your first choice. A timber buyer will measure the standing timber and estimate the volume. The buyer will offer you a price depending on the quality of the timber and the ease of felling and extracting it. If you have good-quality straight-stemmed oak that can be used as saw logs and the woodland has good access and a loading bay, the price will be much higher than a stand of oak that was never high pruned, has large crowns and is a long way from roadside with poor access. Selling standing timber has to allow for the labour of felling and extraction.

Selling felled timber

If you have felled the timber yourself or had a contractor fell the timber, it will now be possible to accurately measure each individual stem. This will also be a time to see the quality of the timber. If the timber has star or ring shake, this will be evident once the timber is felled and will devalue the log considerably.

At this stage, you may have some volume of side branches that can be sold as firewood as well as the main stem for selling as a saw log. A timber buyer will come in at this stage to measure and mark up the stems and then offer a price. If you have measured and marked up the volume of each stem of timber and extracted each of them to a suitable position where they can be collected by a lorry, and the timber is of good quality, the timber should fetch its highest price.

THIS PAGE: A good-quality stem of Douglas fir ready for harvesting.

OPPOSITE: Douglas fir saw logs, measured and ready for sale.

Swing blade mill

Adding value

The value of any tree can be considerably increased by investing time into converting the timber into different products. As a woodlander, there is a balance to be struck with the ratio between the area of woodland you manage to the time you have to add value.

What ratio?

I am often asked: 'How many acres of woodland do I need to earn a living?' There is no simple answer to this question as there are so many variables. What is the stocking rate and quality of the timber? How many days are needed for woodland management activities? What are your skills as a craftsperson to add value? What are your skills at marketing your produce?

If I take the woodland I manage, which is just under 100 acres (about 40ha), a lot of my time is taken up with woodland management activities and therefore I don't have time to add value to all the timber I fell. It makes economic sense to sell some of the timber as raw timber (tax free) and add value to some of the timber to sell as higher-value products.

In another scenario, if a person was managing 5 acres (2ha) of woodland and felled a small amount of timber each year and they had a good level of craft skill, they would have a lot of time to add value to the timber they had felled and it would make economic sense to convert all the timber to higher added-value products.

Sawn timber

Sawing your own timber into planks, posts or beams can be a useful way of adding value. There are a number of different options for milling timber in the woodland and it will depend on the volume of timber you are planning to mill as to whether you invest in a mobile sawmill or you choose to hire in a mobile sawmill and operator to convert the timber into planks. The most basic and cheapest of sawmills is the chainsaw mill.

Chainsaw mill

This is an adapted device that converts your chainsaw into a mill by clamping a frame to the bar and adjusting the sharpening angle of the chain to 15 degrees to create a ripping chain. A ladder is often used to help make the first cut. The ladder is laid on top of the log to be milled and secured to it; the frame of the chainsaw mill runs across the ladder with the chainsaw bar below creating a level cut along the log. With the level cut achieved, the frame can now run across the level cut with the chainsaw bar below it set to whatever thickness of timber you want.

A chainsaw mill can be very useful for milling up timber in very inaccessible parts of the woodland, where extracting the timber is not possible but carrying out the planks is a solution. A chainsaw mill can also be useful where very long beams are needed as the mill is not restricted by the length of a bed like a bandsaw is. Disadvantages can be accuracy of the cutting, wastage of timber (a lot of sawdust is produced because the chain is far thicker than a bandsaw blade) and volume of fuel used.

Chainsaw mill

Swing blade mill

This is a sawmill that uses a circular saw blade, which will turn (swing) through 90 degrees, hence making it possible to mill out dimensioned planks from a log. Different models are available and some have an aluminium frame that can literally be built around a log, making

the mill able to cut timber from logs in inaccessible areas with much more accuracy than the chainsaw mill.

Mobile bandsaw mill

This type of mill is fixed to a trailer. There are many makes and models available – some manual, some hydraulic – and they work by rolling the log onto the trailer bed. The bandsaw runs on rails on the trailer and cuts through the log. These mills can be very accurate in their cutting and, provided the timber to be milled is stacked so that the mobile sawmill can be positioned alongside the timber, a good amount can be milled in a day. A lot of mobile mill owners hire out themselves with the mill on a day rate. About 20 days of hiring yourself and the mill out will pay for a mid-range mobile sawmill, so it doesn't take long to pay for your investment.

*Mobile
bandsaw mill*

Seasoning timber

Having planked up your timber, the timber will be green (unseasoned). You can use the planks green or sell them at this point, or season them and sell them at a higher price as air-dried timber. Kiln drying is used by many timber merchants using dehumidifying kilns, but this is a more industrial process and not suited to adding value in the woodland.

If you are going to air-dry the timber, you will need to store the timber under cover and 'in stick'. 'In stick' is the process of stacking timber planks on top of one another with small sawn softwood sticks placed at intervals between the layers of planks. A piece of slab wood is often used on top of the stack to add weight. Putting timber 'in stick' allows air circulation around the planks and the weight of the stack stops the timber cupping or distorting as it dries.

Timber air-dries at different rates depending on the species of timber, and the thickness and length of the planks. For example, a 1in (25mm) thick x 8ft (2.4m) plank of oak air-dried in stick in a barn will take about two years to reach a moisture content of less than 20%, whereas an alder plank of the same dimensions would take less than a year to reach the same moisture content.

Charcoal

The conversion of wood to charcoal is one of the oldest crafts and can be carried out within the woodland. Traditional earth burns, still carried out in some parts of the world, have been replaced in most industrialized countries by using steel ring kilns or the cleaner burning retort kilns. The process involves the distillation of wood, which, in simple terms, means baking the wood, removing all moisture and ending up with a product that is almost pure carbon. Charcoal needs to be made from seasoned wood not green wood, so you will need to split, stack and cover the wood and come back to convert it to charcoal the following year. Charcoal can be sold as barbecue charcoal, artists' charcoal or the fines (charcoal dust) can be sold as bio-char and used as a soil additive.

Woodchip

Woodchip is both a useful product and a method for clearing unwanted brash. Whether coppicing an area of woodland or thinning a plantation, there is always a large volume of brash to clear away. Traditionally, the brash would be burnt in the woodland but in many woodlands the fire sites are not helpful as they can destroy habitat and ground-cover plants. Some brash can be laid down in the woodland and cross-cut into windrows, but I find chipping some of the volume helps, especially when I am opening up rides or beginning the cut of a new area – it helps create space to fell into.

Chippers can have their own engine, be on wheels, can be self-propelled on tracks or can be attached to a tractor's power take-off (PTO). Some chippers can vary the size of chip produced. The chip can be dried and used as a fuel in woodchip boilers or can be used as a mulch in gardens or around newly planted trees. I often use it on well-trodden paths in the winter, which otherwise would turn to mud and become inaccessible. Whatever your end use, the ability to clear surplus brash makes the woodchipper a useful woodland management tool.

Sawdust

There is sawdust wherever you saw wood. If you operate a sawmill, you will soon build up a large volume of sawdust. If you cross-cut firewood in one area, the volume of sawdust will soon add up. Sawdust can be bagged up and sold to pet stores, or you can compress it and make briquette logs to burn.

OPPOSITE, ABOVE: Oak, air-drying in stick.

OPPOSITE, LOWER: Charcoal burning at Prickly Nut Wood.

RIGHT: A woodchipper converts the large volume of brash into a usable product.

Logs

For many small woodland owners, firewood may be one of the main products sourced from the woodland. Firewood may come from thinning a plantation, side branches from a large standard or coppicing an area of woodland. This material, once felled, will be 'green'. This means it will have a very high moisture content and to turn it into firewood takes time and good practice.

Selling cordwood

If you have more wood than you need for personal use, you may wish to sell it as cordwood. A cord is a well-used forestry measurement for selling small-diameter wood to be converted to logs. A cord measures 4 x 4 x 8ft (1.2 x 1.2 x 2.4m), which equates to 128 cubic feet (3.45 cubic metres) of tightly stacked wood. Firewood merchants will buy wood by the cord and take it away to season, so if you are planning to sell cordwood it is sensible to construct a simple frame to keep the wood off the ground. Think carefully where you stack cordwood as it may be there some time. Pick a spot where it is easy to access with a vehicle and will have good airflow and some sun.

Seasoning firewood

If you wish to season the firewood for your own use, you will need space and time. As wood dries, the moisture escapes through the end grain of the wood, so in order to dry wood well it is important to saw and split it down into smaller-sized pieces. If we take a 4ft (1.2m) length of cordwood and cut it into four pieces 1ft (30cm) long and stack them with good airflow and a gap between the end grain of each log, the wood will dry out much faster than if left in its original size. If we split each of those 1ft (30cm) lengths into two, they again will dry out quicker. Different species of wood all have different drying rates, so, for example, a freshly felled log 1ft (30cm) long and

4in (10cm) diameter of birch or alder will dry out twice as quickly as the same sized freshly felled log of oak.

For logs to burn cleanly and convert the energy efficiently into heat, they must be dried to reduce the moisture content to (currently in the UK) less than 20%.

This can be done manually by seasoning the wood but to reach less than 20% moisture content, it is likely to be a two- to three-year process and will involve having some good dry storage. If you plan on selling logs from your wood, you will need a log shelter or barn with a good airflow to ensure the moisture content reduces sufficiently. You will also need time – I recommend three years.

ABOVE LEFT: Split logs drying in a log shed.
ABOVE RIGHT: Testing the moisture content of a sweet chestnut log at Prickly Nut Wood using a digital moisture meter.
OPPOSITE: Cross-cutting logs using a log holder.

Craftwork

There is a wide range of products that can be made directly from timber felled in your woodland. Most of these products are made from green (unseasoned) wood.

Think about time

If you have felled a lot of timber in a season, it is unlikely that you will have time to convert it all into craft produce. For instance a 12ft (3.65m) x 6in (15cm) stem of birch could be cross-cut into 12 x 1ft (30cm) lengths and then split into quarters, giving 48 billets. Each of these could be made into a spoon. A good spoon carver might manage four a day, so the one 12ft (3.65m) length of birch could take 12 days to turn into craft – and then you need to allow time to market and sell your spoons. If you have 50 12ft (3.65m) lengths of birch and decide to convert it all to spoons, it could take 600 days! This is why many specialist craftspeople buy in their wood.

However, it is possible to strike a balance between the time spent managing, how much of the wood produced is sold as raw material and how much time you dedicate to craftwork.

Making craft in the woodland

When managing coppiced woodlands, some crafts are carried out in the woodland itself. A hurdle maker will often spend a few days cutting hazel, and then convert that hazel into hurdles in the woodland, carrying out the finished product ready to sell. In a chestnut coppice, a pale-fencing maker will cleave, point and peel the pales and carry out the bundles of finished pales. So some craftwork is carried out while managing the woodland but the majority will happen once the winter felling season is over. There is a varied selection of different craft products that can be made directly from timber felled in the woodland. For more information, I would recommend my book *Woodland Craft*.

TABLE OF COMMON COPPICED TREES AND CRAFT USES

NAME OF TREE	CRAFT USE	NAME OF TREE	CRAFT USE
Alder	Charcoal, clog soles, brush heads, spoons, river protection faggots	Hornbeam	Charcoal, firewood, mauls and mallets, wooden cogs
Ash	Furniture, tool handles, hay rakes, gate hurdles, tent pegs, walking sticks, sports equipment, oars, yurts, longbows, spoons, walking sticks, charcoal, firewood	Lime	Carving, spoons, troughs, bast for seat weaving
		Rowan	Walking sticks, spoons, carving
Birch	Besom brooms, horse jumps, bark veneer, shrink pots, charcoal, carving, spoons, firewood	Sweet chestnut	Fencing, palings, buildings, pergolas, arbors, rose arches, roofing shakes, gate hurdles, woven panels, baskets, trugs, gates, walking sticks, yurts, bowls, spoons, faggots, seat weaving bast, charcoal, firewood
Hazel	Hurdles, thatching spars, beanpoles, pea sticks, hedging stakes, binders, garden supports, baskets, rustic furniture, walking sticks, faggots, charcoal, firewood		
		Willow	Basketry, fence panels, artists' charcoal, faggots

A spooncarver using a lap shave to make spoons.

Ollie Moses turning a chestnut bowl on a lathe he made during his apprenticeship at Prickly Nut Wood.

Woodlander's story: crafts at Prickly Nut Wood

At Prickly Nut Wood the year is divided by seasonal activities. Craftwork finds its place as we put down the saws, after the hard but satisfying coppicing season. As the days warm and lengthen, we turn the poles into produce. A lot of the produce, being chestnut, gets turned into fencing and garden products as well as cleaving poles from 1in (2.5cm) to 12in (30cm). It becomes a busy part of our craftwork as poles are peeled and cleft and then fixed or woven into finished products.

Post and rail, palisade, gate hurdles and woven panels, bespoke gates and rustic furniture, roundwood timber frames and roofing shakes all form part of our summer work. Summer brings courses to the woods and, as the days of learning timber framing drift into evenings around the fire, spoons are whittled and stories shared.

Each year I train two apprentices and, as summer days shorten, they often specialize in making a particular product or products of their choice. Rustic furniture, stools, troughs and bowls – each adds their own endeavours to transform the coppiced wood into more products. As the heavy dews of autumn arrive, they head off to coppices new to start their journey as future woodlanders, and I prepare for the next intake and ready myself for winter and the next coppicing season to begin.

OPPOSITE: Top left, a framed cleft chestnut woven panel. Top right, cleft chestnut post-and-rail fencing. Middle left, roundwood cabin. Middle right, chestnut bark used in the film industry. Bottom left, a selection of spoons. Bottom right, chestnut roofing shakes.

Cleaving forms the starting point of many crafts.

NON-TIMBER FOREST PRODUCE

Woodlands can provide a wide range of non-timber forest products that, in many cases, will provide some of the gastronomic pleasures of managing a woodland – but some also offer commercial opportunities.

Forest gardens

These are designed planting schemes that mimic the natural layers of the woodland (see page 92). Originating in the Tropics and pioneered in the UK by the late Robert Hart, forest gardens are now appearing in newly designed and planted woodlands and permaculturally designed landscapes.

Edible layers

In a forest garden, each woodland layer is replaced with an edible or useful species. For example, the canopy might be a plum tree on a Brompton rootstock (creates a large tree); the lower tree layer might be an apple tree on M26 (dwarfing) rootstock; the shrub layer might be a currant or gooseberry; the herbaceous layer could be mint; the ground-cover layer could be strawberries or thyme; the bulb layer could be wild garlic; the climbing layer could be tayberry or kiwi fruit; and the fungi layer inoculated mushroom logs. These are a small example of the many species that can be included in a forest garden. The key to success is diversity, light management and maintenance. In many parts of the Tropics these gardens form a regular part of local food production. In the past 30 years an increasing number of these gardens have been planted in temperate regions.

Creating a forest garden within an existing woodland could be challenging where established trees are likely to cast heavy shade, but the opportunity in large clearings, or particularly to design into new planting schemes, should be considered.

Agroforestry

Agroforestry is a term for where agriculture and forestry combine. The traditional wood pasture systems (see page 16) are well known. Projects involving lines of fruit and nut trees such as apple and walnut and inter-cropping with cereal crops have been trialled in Great Britain. These systems tend to focus primarily on the agricultural side, with the trees planted as a secondary crop and to help with soil stabilization. Any situation where trees are planted among what are usually monocultural cereal crops should be encouraged.

The role of agroforestry in existing woodlands is limited but combining agricultural land and new woodland plantings, where open space could be used to plant annual crops or run livestock while the wood is establishing (and provided the trees are well protected), has great potential.

Abundant apple crop in a Prickly Nut Wood coppice fruit avenue.

Woodlander's story: coppice fruit avenues

Over twenty years ago, I coined the term 'coppice fruit avenues' for some trials I was carrying out in my woodland among the coppice. In hindsight the word 'avenues' was a poor choice – 'clumps' may have been a better term as avenue gives the impression of linear orchards between the cants of coppice.

Although this could be achieved when planting a new woodland, in my woodland, the fruit trees – predominantly apples growing on M11, MM106 and M25 rootstocks (see page 29 for description of rootstocks and their numbers) have been planted in clearings and where standard trees have been felled. The clumps of between five to twelve trees are now well established and produce well where the coppice is cut to the southern side of the

fruit trees. They have to go through barren years, where the coppice grows up and shades the fruit trees and some pruning of coppice stems is sometimes necessary.

Initially, I pruned the fruit trees in a traditional way but have since let them become a bit more wild, only removing branches when the centre of the trees become very congested with intertwining branches. Some of the trees have grown very tall as they have been drawn up by the surrounding coppice. The fruit is often smaller than that of a well-tended fruit tree, but as the majority is turned into apple juice and cider, this is not a problem. Last year, they yielded 125 gallons (568 litres) of juice – not bad for semi-wild apple trees.

Mushroom cultivation

Growing mushrooms on logs within your woodland is a great way of producing a supply of food for your own consumption, but it also provides opportunities for sales of surplus. I have been growing mushrooms on logs for the past 20 years, and my conclusion is that it is easier than you might think!

Keeping it simple

I have picked reliable and easy-to-grow varieties such as shiitake and oyster and avoided varieties that grow in the ground rather than on logs, but in a woodland you should have no shortage of logs, so it makes sense to choose this method. There is a lot of information available about inoculating logs – and inoculation techniques and available mushroom varieties are regularly increasing.

My own methods are simple, but have proved to be successful, so I will share my practice with you. I will use shiitake as my example as it is an easy mushroom to grow. I use mainly sweet chestnut logs but I have had success with a number of other species. I coppice the logs during the dormant winter season and choose logs approximately 5in (12.5cm) diameter, and about 4ft (120cm) long. I choose logs that have been freshly cut no more than six weeks prior to inoculation – logs cut earlier could risk early colonization from wild fungi. I buy in bags of sawdust spawn and keep it refrigerated prior to inoculation. I usually carry out inoculation during March or early April.

The logs are drilled out using a $\frac{1}{2}$in (12mm) drill bit with stop collar. These drill bits are purposely designed for inoculating logs and create a hole that is the perfect depth for inserting the sawdust spawn using a brass inoculator. The holes are drilled around the log at approximately 6in (15cm) apart. Once the log is drilled, the sawdust spawn is inserted using the inoculator. The spawn is then sealed with a food wax. This is heated up and dabbed on with a small paint brush. I use a food-grade wax, similar to what is used to seal cheeses. The first year I inoculated logs I used beeswax, but my bees decided to strip all the wax off the logs and take it back!

Once the logs are inoculated, I stand them, leaning at about a 60-degree angle, in a damp, shady part of the woodland. It is important the logs do not dry out, so avoid direct sunlight. With sweet chestnut logs I leave them for about 18 months, by which time the mycelium will have colonized the log and we will be heading into autumn. The rain and change of season from the summer's warmth will naturally encourage the logs to fruit and a first crop of mushrooms will emerge.

The following year, from spring, I can take a few logs and throw them in my pond. I leave them there for two days and then take them out and place them back in their original position – about one week later a crop of mushrooms will appear. This process of shocking the logs by immersing them in water can be carried out three times during the year. So, having shocked them and harvested a crop, I rest them for a couple of months before shocking them again. This process maximizes the yield out of each log. This can be carried on for a few years until the log is decomposing.

Mushrooms fruiting on inoculated logs.

Inoculating chestnut logs with shiitake mushroom spawn at Prickly Nut Wood.

Meat as a by-product

At a time in our history where climate change dictates we reduce farming of meat due to its large-scale methane production, wild meat from the woodland offers an alternative source to farmed meat. In harvesting this meat and keeping population numbers in balance, you can feel comfortable knowing the meat on your plate is there as part of a management plan that ensures the successful growing of trees.

Deer

Deer numbers have increased dramatically over the past 30 years and the number of introduced species breeding in the wild have increased. Deer, in balanced numbers, can live within a silvicultural system – it is when those numbers get very high that the impact and damage in woodland increases. Especially at risk are newly planted trees, natural regeneration and coppice regrowth.

At Prickly Nut Wood, there are native roe deer, large herds of migratory fallow deer (many of which escaped from a deer farm after the 1987 storm that flattened the fencing around them) and the, small in physical size but ever-increasing in numbers, muntjac. The culling of deer is well regulated under the Deer Act in Great Britain, but with the engagement of a qualified deer stalker, the benefit of a fine supply of wild venison, low in fat and with no added antibiotics, can provide an ethical source of meat with the knowledge you are reducing the impact of grazing on young trees.

However, it seems we are slow to learn lessons from the past. Not far from Prickly Nut Wood, a deer farm has sprung up, farming deer to supply venison to one of the large supermarket chains. This farm is farming red deer, a very large deer species and one that is not found in the south-east of England in the wild. I have inspected their fencing and, with large trees around some of the perimeter, we are one storm away from introducing red deer to the woodlands of the south-east. With deer numbers needing more control in local woodlands, it should be wild venison not farmed venison that finds its way into the food chain.

Wild boar

Wild boar became extinct in the Middle Ages in Great Britain, but in the 1980s wild boar farms sprang up with dangerous animal licences to allow the breeding of the boar for meat. Naturally, many escaped and now there are growing populations occurring throughout Great Britain. One area where they have seemed to have become well established is the Forest of Dean. Wild boar are native to Great Britain and deserve their place amongst our forests. But like all species with no natural predators, their numbers will need to be kept in balance and this again offers an opportunity to supply wild rather than farmed meat into the food chain.

Rabbit

Rabbits, once well established in an area, can cause a lot of damage to coppice regrowth (particularly hazel) and natural regeneration. I grew up eating a lot of rabbit. Ferreting was a childhood activity and you learnt to skin and gut along with reading and writing. Rabbit is a flavoursome meat but seems somewhat out of fashion as a friend of mine found out. He asked his local butcher for one, who told him that he might be able to source one from France! Remember, it is legally your responsibility to control rabbits on your land in England and Wales.

Grey squirrel

The grey squirrel is one of the most damaging creatures of broadleaved trees in England. Its ability to ring-bark trees has been particularly detrimental to new beech woodlands. If, like myself, you have to take responsibility for controlling grey squirrel numbers, then it makes sense to eat the meat.

Grey squirrel meat is surprisingly good, but fiddly to skin and prepare. Most of the meat is on the back legs with a little on the front and saddle. With the introduction of contraceptives to control grey squirrels, I will reluctantly be removing the meat from my wild food supply.

Wood pigeon

Although not a problem to the woodland itself, wood pigeons do attack my brassicas if they get a chance! But my main reason for shooting a few pigeons each year is that pigeon breast is one of my favourite wild foods. Lightly pan-fried, it is a delicacy for the most discerning woodlander.

Pheasant and game birds

While I appreciate shoots are an important part of the rural economy and the main income for some woodlands, the idea of standing in a line shooting birds that are being flushed out to fly in front of you does nothing for me. Hunting, like fishing to me, is about fieldcraft, the quiet approach to stalk and kill your dinner is a mindset that takes focus and time, accepting there will be days when you return with nothing. That is not to say I do not enjoy taking a few pheasants as they pass through the woodland, but I have to stalk them and give them a fairer chance of survival.

OPPOSITE: Red deer stag in the woods.
ABOVE LEFT: Wild boar.
ABOVE RIGHT: Pheasant.

THIS PAGE: Chestnuts
in a chestnut basket.
Autumn at Prickly
Nut Wood.

OPPOSITE: Chicken
of the woods appears
throughout summer on
old chestnut stools.

Foraging

Foraging is a great pleasure in a woodland, not only because it can provide the enjoyment of
unusual wild food but also that it helps with your identification skills of plants and fungi. I have
been foraging and trying different wild foods at Prickly Nut Wood for the past 30 years and I now
define foraging into two categories: wild food and survival food. Wild food consists of the plants
and fungi that I forage and enjoy each year such as chanterelles, horn of plenty, chicken of the
woods, wild garlic, wood sorrel, lime leaves, chestnuts and billberries.

Survival food consists of plants and fungi that I know
I can identify and eat but would only choose to in a survival
situation. These are plants and fungi such as cleavers, rose
bay willow herb, acorns, jew's ears and honey fungus.

Be clear about your identification before trying foraged
foods. There are courses you can go on to help with
identification and follow the rule – if you are not sure then
don't eat it! Over time you will try a variety of different
wild foods from your woodland and know the ones you
enjoy and the ones you don't.

Nuts

Living in a predominantly chestnut woodland, during the
first two to three weeks of October, the annual abundant
chestnut harvest arrives. These flavoursome nuts can be
ground to a flour that has formed a staple in parts of Europe.
There are so many recipes and uses for sweet chestnuts.
The abundant volume of nuts, and the spiky nut cases, which
keep squirrels at bay until the nut is fully ripe and the case
ready to open, makes this a food we should be utilizing more.

The difficulty with marketing English chestnuts is that
they are smaller than the large grafted varieties that fill the
supermarket shelves from Italy and Spain each autumn.
The challenge with chestnuts is in peeling them, and the

larger imported nuts give more nut-flesh for each nut peeled. My secret to peeling them is to steam them. Using a knife, place a slit through the skin to allow the steam in and to create a place to start peeling from. Steam them for twenty minutes and then wrap them in a tea towel to keep them warm. Peel them as soon as they are not too hot to handle and the skin and membrane should come away fairly easily.

Hazelnuts are often devoured by grey squirrels before they are ripe. Without the chestnut's spiky protective case, they are easy prey. Commercial hazelnuts (both cobnuts and filberts) are usually grown in orchards known as platts. These are often in an open field situation so that the platt is not easily accessible for squirrels moving from tree to tree.

Walnuts are also usually grown in orchards, but individual trees can often be found on the edge of woodlands and provide a useful crop for the forager. Many exotic walnuts

such as the heartnut and butternut are now being planted in Great Britain. The black walnut is the most recommended if you want the dual purpose of good-quality timber and a nut crop.

The monkey puzzle is a good tree to plant for future nut crops. Patience is needed as it may be more than 50 years before it starts producing. Both male and female trees are needed so it is worth planting a few. Fifty years may seem like a long time but if you are planting a new woodland, why not try some monkey puzzle standards over hazel coppice? You will be leaving a food legacy for future generations. When the trees do start cropping they produce an abundance of very good-flavoured nuts. I remember harvesting a good crop from some mature monkey puzzles growing on the west coast of Scotland.

Medicinal plants, saps, dyes and seed collection

A friend of mine who is a practising herbalist has harvested small quantities of medicinal herbs from my woods. This has been a symbiotic process with myself gaining more knowledge about their uses in return for the plant material.

I have tapped the sap of birch, sycamore and field maple to make wine. The sap of these trees can be tapped just prior to spring when the sap begins to flow and life is returning to the near-dormant trees. Do not expect to get a sweet sap, similar to maple syrup. The sugar maple relies on the freezing winters of parts of North America and Canada and has a naturally higher sugar content in its sap. Sugar maple has a sap with a sugar content of around 2%. To create the sweet maple syrup you can buy in the UK it has been reduced by one fortieth. So it takes 40 gallons (182 litres) of fresh sugar maple sap to make 1 gallon of maple syrup.

With silver birch, the sugar content of the sap is around 0.5–1% sugar content. So it would take 80–160 gallons (364–728 litres) of birch sap to produce 1 gallon (4.5 litres) of sweet birch syrup! I tap a few birches each year and ferment the sap (with added sugar or honey) to make birch sap wine. It is a wine that is tapped just before the arrival of spring and ready to drink as autumn arrives. It is a good wine for marking the changing of the seasons.

A number of woodland trees and plants produce dyes for dying fabric and wool. Elder, alder, birch and walnut are tried and tested trees with dyeing properties.

Seed collection should be considered in any woodland. You may be planning to use tree seed to grow on into whips to plant or sell, you may be direct seeding in areas that need more young trees or you may be harvesting seed to supply to a local tree nursery.

OPPOSITE: Tapping a silver birch tree in spring to collect the sap for wine making.

A WILD FOOD FORAGING DIARY

Here are some of the tastier foraging foods I have found in Prickly Nut Wood, in surrounding woods and on local footpaths.

SPRING
Wild garlic, nettle, chickweed, wood sorrel, salad burnet, jack by the hedge, mint, hawthorn leaves, lime leaves, birch sap, squirrel, venison.

SUMMER
Chickweed, mint, elderflower, wood sorrel, bilberries, pennywort, wild marjoram, wild strawberry, chicken of the woods, chanterelles, blackberries, wood pigeon, squirrel, venison.

AUTUMN
Chestnuts, hazelnuts, walnuts, apples, sloes, giant puffballs, ceps, horn of plenty, rosehips, elderberries, wood pigeon, squirrel, venison.

WINTER
Bittercress, wood sorrel, wild garlic, wood blewit, pheasant, wood pigeon, rabbit, squirrel, venison.

THIS PAGE: Wild garlic is mainly foraged for its leaves, but the flowers make a good addition to a salad.

OPPOSITE: A foraged salad of lime leaves, hawthorn leaves, wild garlic and wood sorrel.

Bees

Bees should be considered in a woodland as long as they can be kept in an area that is not too overshaded with large trees. Another important consideration will be whether there is enough diversity of species to keep a nectar flow available for the bees from early spring through to late autumn. Woodlands that are quite monocultural in nature may be unsuitable for siting a hive.

Sources of nectar

At Prickly Nut Wood, the first nectar flow of the year comes from the pussy willow, followed by the plum, pear and apple blossom. A few exotic acers provide a good flow, and bluebell and gorse are out early. Bramble and soft fruit soon follow as well as dandelion and a number of herbs in my garden. I planted a lot of small-leaved lime about 25 years ago – this produces a feast for the bees and is soon followed by the prolific chestnut flower throughout the woodland.

Clover is available in fields adjacent to the wood and wild and cultivated flowers keep the bees going until the ivy flowers emerge, which brings the cycle to an end for winter. This variety of nectar available throughout the seasons when bees are most active and flying ensures a rich, dark and well-flavoured honey.

Top bar hives

I have kept bees at Prickly Nut Wood for a number of years and have recently started using top bar hives. I keep bees predominantly for their pollination of my fruit trees and for their own survival. As much as I love honey, I am happy to take less honey and focus on building up a strong colony. One advantage with a top bar is that the bees make their own wax comb, so if you are making products from beeswax you get a very good-quality wax.

ABOVE: Pussy willow produces early woodland pollen for bees.
OPPOSITE: A top bar hive positioned to pollinate a coppice fruit avenue at Prickly Nut Wood.

SOCIAL
FORESTRY

Social forestry is a term that covers all areas of working with woodlands where the woodlands are providing the space and connection for groups of people to carry out a variety of activities. In many of these cases, the goal is for social benefit rather than individual gain.

LEFT Adult education – a roundwood timber framing course at Prickly Nut Wood.

OPPOSITE: Education through forest schools and bushcraft is a growth area in social forestry.

Education

Woodlands offer a great opportunity for inspirational education. Away from the confines of our institutional buildings, students young and old can benefit from the natural landscape and healthy properties that an outdoor educational experience can offer.

Adult education and wellbeing

Forests offer many opportunities for adult education, through craft courses, woodland management, natural building and much more. These courses are, of course, educational, but offer more to the student than a traditional classroom. The opportunity to spend time with a group of like-minded people, learning new skills and absorbing the calm and healing of the woodland, has a very positive impact on our well-being.

I notice, in particular with a four-day course, how students arrive, often quite hyperactive from their journey. As each day passes, they relax, slow down and interact more thoughtfully with one another. The ability of the woodland to provide a calm and revitalizing environment will, I am sure, play an increasing part in our future. Woodlands have rightly been identified as good places for people suffering with mental health issues. In the past I have worked with the charity Mind, having groups working in the woodland. Again, it is the environment as much as the activity that creates a positive outcome.

Forest schools

The growth of forest schools is one of the most positive developments in social forestry in the UK. The importance of offering children engagement with the forest environment at a young age could have long-term positive consequences for how future decision-makers view the natural world. It is the current generation of children, attending forest school today, who will have to make crucial decisions on climate change, try to reverse the damage done and map out a new way of living.

Walks and talks

Other educational opportunities in woodland involve nature walks, identifying plants and birds, to enjoy the sounds of the dawn chorus or perhaps an evening bat walk. Bushcraft courses are made to be taught in a woodland environment and are an educational growth area. Courses in art and photography can again be all the more enhanced by the location.

Shelter creates a meeting point in the woodland and can be multifunctional in its uses.

Community forestry

Community forestry can take a number of forms, from a group of people buying woodland shares, then managing and sharing any profits from the woodland together, through to a community woodland owned by a trust and managed by volunteers from the local community. There are many variants around these two models but the key component is a group of people working or managing wood for a collective rather than individual goals.

Large-scale community forests

Community forests can be large scale; these are often dictated by government policy in re-foresting a particular area of the country; many of these have been established around large towns and cities, offering residents an important connection with nature. Often they set up one or a number of focal points offering volunteering opportunities, tree planting, forest school and adult craft education.

Smaller-scale community forests

Kilfinan Community Forest is an example of where the community has taken over the management and future of its local forest. The small community of Tighnabruaich on the Argyle peninsula has seen a steady population decline over the past 50 years. Kilfinan Community Forest is a registered Scottish charity and social enterprise that now owns 1,300 acres (561ha) of forest, much of which was previously owned by the Forestry Commission. The project is breathing life back into the community, offering education, employment and long-term housing. This, in turn, is bringing more people into the local community.

The charity provides forest school education, offers youth skills development and work experience for 16–18 year olds. The forest has its own sawmill, providing timber for local needs and for house building. Logs and other forest products provide additional sales and there are currently four paid staff involved with both administration and practical forestry. Housing needs are provided through forest crofts. This encourages new people into the community with the opportunity to live and work in the forest. Community composting, allotments and a series of pathways for walking, cycling and horses have all been established. This project contains all the elements that show a model for future community forests.

RIGHT: A classroom in the woodland, built from the woodland, to learn more about the woodland.

OPPOSITE: Autumn leaf-fall draws more people into the woods for walks and recreation.

Hiring and events

Woodland events can take on many forms, from corporate days out and launch events to weddings, funerals and even outdoor theatre. They can be tailored to suit many different ideas, and can prove to be a memorable and moving experience for all involved.

Shoots and corporate events

Many woodland owners earn income through shooting. These corporate events can produce a steady income and, provided the event is well managed, (i.e. with repeat bookings, forming a relationship with shooting syndicates and becoming part of their annual calendar), they can ensure a stable return from the woodland. Many shoots are run by larger estates, where gamekeepers and bird rearing are part of the land management strategy, all gearing up for the main shoots during the late autumn/winter season.

Other corporate events in woodland can be more bespoke to a company's needs. Utilizing the woodland 'space' as an occasional corporate venue can bring in much-needed income to then be utilized on woodland management activities or purchasing tools and equipment to help facilitate the management of the woodland.

Weddings, funerals and life events

Woodlands offer a wonderful setting for weddings and a reflective space for funerals or other life events for those of us who are looking for something a little different. The growth of woodlands as a venue for special events is growing. There are a number of woodlands that specialize in weddings, often providing the woodland venue and accommodation in yurts, tipis and bell tents, or providing an adjacent field for camping.

Green burial sites have sprung up in woodlands and fields across Great Britain. These often start as a greenfield site where each burial has a tree planted – over time, a whole woodland is created. Usually there are no headstones or markers, just a Global Positioning System (GPS) record of the burial site. This allows the woodland to evolve with a more natural feel than that of a graveyard. Over time, the woodland will mature and, as generations pass and those who have passed away begin to be forgotten, anyone tracing an ancestor's passing place will be able to find the spot via GPS.

The Shakespeare's oak at Prickly Nut Wood.

Woodlander's story: Shakespeare's oak

I have been involved with a few corporate days in the woods where I have facilitated environmental businesses, who have used the day as an opportunity to get staff out of the office and into the natural environment. Other days have been more specific, with architect firms and wildlife charities keen to focus on the woodland management and biodiversity at Prickly Nut Wood. Corporate days can be varied and the most diverse have involved creating a space for inspiration and have used the woodland environment alongside musicians, artists and alternative practitioners interspersed with brainstorming ideas. One produced a performance of *A Midsummer Night's Dream* and named the veteran oak at Prickly Nut Wood, 'Shakespeare's oak'. Its acorns were potted up and given out to people to plant at a performance at the Globe Theatre in London.

Zip wires and canopy walks are proving very popular for outdoor exercise.

Recreation

The opportunities for recreation in woodlands are growing and, although in most cases this is positive, some caution should be considered when looking at the long-term impact to the woodland. Plantations and more recently planted woodlands are likely to be better choices for recreational activities than ancient woodland, where human traffic through the woodlands should be more controlled.

Sensitive engagement

Prickly Nut Wood is ancient semi-natural woodland and a site of special scientific interest (SSSI) and although I have targeted days when I have groups visiting the woodland, they keep to the main hard ride and the more sensitive areas of the woodland are left undisturbed. Managing recreational activities in a woodland should take a similar approach, assessing the woodland and designing a plan of where recreational activities could work and where they should be more restricted. Here are options and types of activities to consider:

Access

Your woodland may already have public access through footpaths, bridleways or right-to-roam legislation. If you wish to open up your woodland to the public, agreement can be reached as part of a Forestry Commission plan or via your local authority in England to open a permissive path. Permissive paths allow public access through your woodland on a chosen route but can be closed off and do not have the same highways rights as a public footpath or bridleway. The Forestry Commission's Woodland Carbon Fund pays grants for extraction roads to be created in new woodlands, which also have public usage.

Accessibility for wheelchairs in woodlands has been slowly improving with nature reserves and the Woodland Trust beginning to create accessible pathways. But there is much more that can still be achieved to open up woodland access for wheelchair users.

Cycling

Woodlands can offer cycling access by creating a good cycle path through the woodland or by linking the woodland with larger plans for the cycling network. Unmade-up paths offer mountain biking opportunities and some areas of woodland have created pathways and jumps, giving a whole mountain bike trail experience, and charge per visit to use the facility.

Paintballing

Paintball activities in woodland have grown over the last 20 years and there are now both large activity centres and small-scale woodland games sites. It is best suited to poor-quality woodland and can be restricted so that the activities are kept to quite a small area.

Canopy access, zip wires and rope walks

There are a number of companies that have set up successful woodland canopy access, creating rope access, canopy swings and zip wires through the forest. Although this is a specialist field, if you have the right woodland and enough parking this could be worth considering as a recreational use, as there seems currently to be a high demand.

Biosecurity precautions

With all recreational activities, biosecurity controls should be in place. The more human activity that happens within a woodland, the more accelerated the risk of spreading tree diseases. An educational awareness programme should be introduced for all recreational woodlands, and biosecurity precautions of washing footwear before entering the woodland for recreation should become the normal response rather than being seen as overcautious.

ABOVE: Walking down a woodland ride, you are at risk of carrying tree diseases if you do not wash your boots after each walk.

BELOW: A mountain bike track with jumps and different levels of difficulty provides an income from this plantation woodland.

Camping

The opportunity to do some wild camping is one of the benefits of owning a woodland and part of the reason for the recent rise in demand for small woodlands.

Within a small woodland, you can set up camp and get a taste of the wild, and enjoy and learn about the night-time activities of owls and badgers. Combined with woodland management activities and craftwork during the day, this is an appealing part of owning a woodland for families. This cannot be a commercial activity (see section on planning law), but it does allow you and friends to enjoy staying overnight in the woodland for up to 28 days a year.

Wild camping

It is possible in Scotland to 'wild camp' in woodlands, provided you follow the Scottish outdoor access code. In the rest of Great Britain, you need the landowner's permission. In Dartmoor National Park there are areas that are designated for one or two nights' wild camping provided you are on foot and just with a backpack. These opportunities are not for family-sized tents or camper vans.

Over the past 20 years, camping has evolved from simple nights in a tent you carry with you, into – for many – arriving with half the contents of a bedroom and kitchen and setting up a major encampment. If the latter is how you like to camp then campsites provide the opportunity for you to camp this way, with toilets, showers, rubbish collection and often a shop.

If you wish to wild camp in woodlands, a simple, minimalistic approach is recommended. The key to wild camping in woodlands is to leave no trace of your time there, and to take away whatever you brought with you.

Travel light if you plan on wild camping.

THE WOODLAND SPACE

The value of woodlands as a place of well-being and recreation is just beginning to be recognized. There will be many opportunities for woodland owners as the demand to access woodlands and the healthy environment they offer increases. The challenge will be in finding the balance so that sensitive woodlands with diverse flora and fauna are kept to a minimum of human traffic whereas recently established woodlands and those of less biodiverse importance can accommodate more people.

This, of course, takes us back to woodland assessment (see page 34). Taking time to assess a woodland properly will help enable the right choices for a particular woodland. Timber production, recreation and increasing biodiversity can all be achieved within one woodland but the planning and control of human traffic need careful planning and consideration.

The appreciation of woodlands as a place of well-being is on the increase.

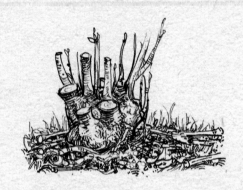

WOODLAND OWNERSHIP

This chapter looks at the opportunities for purchasing woodland and what to be aware of when buying a woodland, but also considers future scenarios for the next generation of young woodlanders.

Buying or gaining access to woodland

For many people the opportunity of buying a woodland may be a lifelong dream. For others, it may always be out of reach, but if you are keen to work in the woods, opportunities can be found through training and buying cutting rights.

Woodland agents and sizing

Woodlands can be purchased through specialist estate agents who sell woodlands and often also farms and other agricultural land. The price of commercial woodland, as with houses in the UK, varies depending on where in the country the woodland for sale is situated.

There are also a number of estate agents who have appeared in the last ten years who sell small areas of woodland targeting the leisure market. Usually they have a large area of woodland to sell and break it down into smaller compartments that they sell off individually. I refer to this approach as 'woodlotting'. This approach has advantages and disadvantages.

The advantages are that with smaller areas of woodland being sold, it allows people who would not be able to afford a larger woodland an opportunity to purchase a small area. Another advantage is the possibility to share resources and labour where there are major work activities to carry out.

The disadvantages are that as there is a demand for these small parcels of woodland, it has inflated the prices to twice or even three times the value per acre of commercial woodland. These small parcels of woodland often come with restrictive covenants and usually shared access with a number of other woodland owners, which can cause controversy. The woodlands themselves are often broadleaf ancient semi-natural woodlands that have had a pattern of management for hundreds of years. Once sold they are carved up into individual pieces with different owners all carrying out their own interests on their own pieces of land. This can have a negative effect on biodiversity.

Where these woodlots work is where the owners form a core group and draw up a management plan for the whole woodland. This treats it as one woodland, although individuals own their own plots within that woodland.

Direct sales

Often the best way to purchase woodland is by a direct sale. This is where the seller and buyer are known to each other. This hopefully means that there is already a good degree of trust between buyer and seller and if, for instance, the seller is a farmer selling off an area of woodland, they may feel happier selling to someone they know who will become a future landowning neighbour. I purchased my land this way. The advantages are that you can both avoid expensive agent's fees. Once you have agreed a price and are both happy to proceed, the buyer can engage a solicitor to act only for the buyer in preparing the transfer, presenting it to the seller to review, approve and sign for completion. The solicitor will of course advise the seller of their right to take independent legal advice. This is the cheapest way to transact a sale, with the buyer paying the full solicitor's costs – this can also be attractive to the seller.

Alternatively, the solicitor can act for you as buyer and arrange for another solicitor in another office of their firm to represent the seller if he or she would like some representation, but they will only consider doing this if there is no conflict between the seller and buyer about the transaction. The seller and buyer would both be liable for their respective solicitor's costs, but the overall costs are likely to be cheaper than engaging solicitors from different firms, which is another option.

THIS PAGE: A hard ride at Prickly Nut Wood.

LEFT: Ferns emerging in spring alongside a woodland stream.

Searches

Whether you are engaging a solicitor or carrying out your own searches, you will need to ensure you are purchasing the land without inherited issues. This will involve carrying out a local authority search for any records held against the land and the Land Registry title. If you are buying a piece of woodland that is to be separated from the existing whole Land Registry title of the seller, then it will be important to agree and search for any issues there may be around the access you will gain to the land. You will need to have environmental searches for land contamination and look into any legal contracts that apply to the land that will need to be transferred to the new owner, such as an existing Woodland Grant Scheme contract with the Forestry Commission. This will include any third-party occupants of the land who may have an agreement to use the land for a particular activity. One area that is very important to check is that you are buying the shooting and mineral rights for the woodland as part of the purchase.

Forestry Commission woodland

The Forestry Commission, or rather Forestry England, Forestry and Land Scotland, Natural Resources Wales and the Forest Service (Northern Ireland) 'owns' over 2.1 million acres (860,000 ha) of woodland. I have placed 'owns' in inverted commas as the woodland does, in fact, belong to the public and is administered by the Government, which

RIGHT: Good-quality hazel coppice awaiting the next generation of coppice workers.

OPPOSITE: Matching derelict coppice and young people wanting a 'woodlanders' lifestyle could be a symbiotic relationship for the Forestry Commission in England.

was caught by surprise when it tried to sell off part of the public's woodland estate into private hands in 2010.

These woodlands have 'right to roam' public access and the Government, under public pressure, U-turned and accepted that the forestry estate should remain in public ownership. There are areas of the forest estate that are unmanaged and these are often mixed broadleaf or overstood coppice woodlands.

Matching land with young woodlanders

One option that should be considered is that these areas could be leased to young people who are keen to work and restore these coppice woodlands. The lease would keep the woodlands open to public access but would give the young foresters an opportunity to work and earn a living from land they could not afford to buy. Low-impact housing could be tied in with the lease (possibly similar to the crofting housing scheme offered by Kilfinan Community Forest) as well as support from the regional forestry office in drawing up management plans for the woodland areas. This would increase biodiversity by restoring derelict woodland and offer livelihood opportunities for the next generation.

Buying standing coppice

Traditionally, large estates that owned areas of coppice woodland would sell the standing coppice by auction. By buying the standing coppice, the coppice worker would buy the rights to cut and make use of the coppice poles but have no rights to the land. This process continues today but rarely uses auctions. There are a number of estates that will sell the standing coppice to a coppice worker via a private agreement. It usually helps to be known to the estate or referred by someone with a good reputation in the industry. Once established as a reliable coppice worker, many find themselves with a continual supply of coppice from the one estate and the cost of buying the standing coppice should be able to be recouped in the first week of work by a good coppice worker.

AGRICULTURAL LAND

If you are unable to find suitable woodland to purchase, it is well worth considering buying agricultural land and planting it up as woodland. Poor or degraded agricultural land can often be purchased at a better price than woodland. Often this land will be greatly improved by planting trees, especially by adding nitrogen-fixing species such as alder. There will be grants available for planting the woodland and the process of planting and seeing a woodland grow from saplings to canopy cover in twenty years is a very satisfying feeling, especially that of knowing you are leaving a legacy for future generations.

Glossary

Acid soil Soil with a pH value of usually less than 5.5.

Agroforestry A combination of agricultural and forestry use on the same piece of land.

Alkaline soil Soil with a pH value of usually greater than 8.5.

Base-rich soil Soil that is rich in basic ions (typically calcium and magnesium).

Bast Fibrous inner bark of a tree (phloem or vascular tissue of a plant).

Binders Thin flexible rods of coppiced material (often hazel), used for weaving between stakes on a laid hedge.

Biodiversity The variety of plant and animal life in a particular habitat.

Biomass Plant or animal material used for energy production (heat and electricity).

Biomass forestry Forestry practice targeted to produce biomass.

Bletted The ripening and softening of certain fruits to make them more edible – happens naturally by frost but can be done artificially.

Boreal A climatic zone related to Earth's northern regions.

Brash Small branches from the side and top of a tree.

Broadleaf A tree or plant with wide flat leaves.

Bronze Age Prehistoric period that followed the Stone Age and preceded the Iron Age.

Canopy The upper layer in mature tree crowns, including all biological organisms that inhabit that layer.

Capstan A broad revolving cylinder with a vertical axis, used for winding a rope or cable.

Cant A defined area of coppice.

Chisel plough A soil tillage device pulled by a tractor or animal, used to break up soil underground without turning it.

Cleavers Selected rods to be split into two separate mirrored pieces.

Climax species In a forest, these are the tree species that remain unchanged in terms of species composition, until they are disturbed by natural occurrences such as extreme wind or forest fire.

Commoner A person who has 'rights of common' over common land or over another's land. This might be for grazing or firewood collection, for example.

Coniferous Trees and shrubs with cone-bearing seeds.

Coombe A short valley or hollow on a hillside, particularly in southern England.

Crown The branches and top of the tree above the main stem.

Deciduous A tree that loses its leaves in the autumn and grows new ones in the spring.

Drift A row of cut coppice poles all laid in the same direction.

Earthbank A bank or mound of earth, often defining an old boundary or woodland edge.

Epicormic Of a tree shoot or branch growing from a previously dormant bud on the trunk or branch of a tree.

Epiphytic From epiphyte, an organism that grows on the surface of a plant and derives its moisture and nutrients from the air, rain, water or from accumulated debris surrounding it.

Etherings Another word for **binders**.

Extraction rides Woodland paths and tracks that are used for the principal purpose of extracting timber.

Faggots Tied bundles of small branches traditionally used to fire ovens, now used for riverbank restoration and coastal defence.

Fauna All the animal life present in a particular region or time.

Ferreting Using ferrets to flush out rabbits from their burrows and drive them into nets.

Flora All the plant life present in a particular region or time.

Grafting Horticultural technique where plant tissues are joined together to fuse as one plant.

Heeling-in Temporarily digging in plants so that the roots are covered to avoid frost damage before being moved to their final planting position.

Herbaceous Vascular plants that have no persistent woody stems above ground.

High forest Consists of large, tall mature trees with a closed canopy.

Ice Age period of time where glaciers covered a large part of Earth's surface.

Indicator plant A plant that thrives only under particular environmental conditions and therefore indicates these conditions where it is found.

Invertebrates Any animal that lacks a vertebral column or backbone.

Megafauna Comprises the large or giant animals of an area, habitat or geological period.

Mast year A year in which trees produce a large crop of seed.

Native species Species of indigenous origin that have developed, occurred naturally or existed for many years in an area.

Notch planting A fast method for planting young whips by opening a notch in the ground with a spade.

On-cycle With reference to coppice, the trees are cut on the optimum cycle in years to be productive.

Overbark Measurement taken before the bark has been removed.

Overstood Coppice that has been allowed to grow beyond its optimum cycle in years.

Pales Small cleft pieces of wood, usually sweet chestnut.

Paling Fencing made up of chestnut pales that are wired together – comes in a roll.

pH A scale used to measure the acidity or alkalinity of a substance.

Pioneer species Fast-growing, free-seeding species that first appear in naturally regenerating woodland.

Ratchet Mechanical device consisting of a toothed wheel or rack engaged with a pawl that permits it to move in one direction only.

Revetment Sloping structures placed on banks or cliffs to absorb the energy of incoming water.

Ride (see extraction ride).

Ring-bark The process of removing bark around the circumference of a tree to cut off the flow of sap and cause the tree to die above the point it is ring barked.

Rods Small-diameter coppice poles.

Rootstock A plant onto which another variety is grafted.

Seedbank A store of dormant seed.

Silviculture The practice of growing and cultivating trees.

Silvopastoral The practice of integrating trees, forage and grazing livestock in a mutually beneficial way.

Snedding Removing side branches and the top of a felled tree.

Spokeshave A hand tool with a blade that takes off very thin layers of wood.

Standard A single-stemmed tree allowed to grow mature, commonly amongst coppice.

Star shake/ring shake Defects that are found in felled timber that can make the timber unsellable. Star shake is caused by extreme heat or severe frost and ring shake by twisting in high winds.

Steam bending Woodworking technique where wood is exposed to steam to make it pliable and is clamped to a former to create a new shape as it cools.

Stem Main trunk of a tree.

Subsoiler (see chisel plough).

Succession The process of how a woodland evolves naturally from a field to climax woodland.

Sward Portion of ground covered in grass.

Temperate Relating to or denoting a region or climate characterized by mild temperatures.

Undercut The drawing of a horizontal blade through the soil at a certain depth below a bed of young trees in a tree nursery to sever the deeper roots and encourage a more fibrous root system.

Undergrazed Where livestock graze pasture below trees.

Underwood Another word for coppice.

Weavers Rods chosen for their flexibility to be woven into a hedge or panel.

Windrows Rows of brash that have been cut into small pieces to aid its decomposition.

Windthrow An area of woodland that has been blown over by the wind.

Zales Upright rods in a hurdle or panel around which weavers are woven.

ABOUT THE AUTHOR

Ben Law, woodsman, craftsman, eco-builder, teacher and writer, lives and works in Prickly Nut Wood in West Sussex, UK. The building of his unique woodland home was featured on Channel 4's *Grand Designs* in the UK and was voted by viewers as the most popular episode ever. In addition to the coppicing of his own woodland, he runs courses on sustainable woodland management and permaculture, runs a specialist eco-building company and trains apprentices. He has written many books, including *Woodland Craft* (GMC Publications, 2015), *Woodland Workshop* (GMC Publications, 2018), *The Woodland House* (Permanent Publications, 2005), *The Woodland Year* (Permanent Publications, 2008), and *Woodsman: Living in a Wood in the 21st Century* (HarperCollins, 2013).

www.ben-law.co.uk

Publisher **Jonathan Bailey**
Production **Jim Bulley, Jon Hoag**
Senior Project Editor **Virginia Brehaut**
Copy Editor **Robin Pridy**
Designer **Cathy Challinor**
Illustrator **Jane Bottomley**
Cover Illustration **Celia Hart**

All photographs by Ben Law, except:
Andrew Perris on pages: 2, 3, 8, 9, 20, 21, 22, 32, 33, 39 (left), 40
(third in sequence), 41 (second and fourth from last, in sequence),
44, 50, 61, 94 (lower, middle), 96, 97, 102, 103, 109, 127, 136 (middle
left and lower left), 138, 139, 153, 155, 160, 161, 169, 178, 179, 180,
and 184. Shutterstock.com on pages: 35 (lower), 40 (all except third,
seventh and ninth in sequence), 41 (all except second and fourth
from last, in sequence), 43 (lower), 45 (right), 46, 47, 58, 59, 147, and
159 (all). Alamy.com on pages: 40 (ninth in sequence) and 142.

Colour origination by GMC Reprographics
Printed and bound in China

Index

To order a book, contact:
GMC Publications Ltd
Castle Place, 166 High Street, Lewes,
East Sussex, BN7 1XU,
United Kingdom
Tel: +44 (0)1273 488005
www.gmcbooks.com